Who's RAISING your Child?

Battling the Marketers for Your Child's Heart and Soul

Who's Raising Your Child?

Published by the Boys Town Press
Father Flanagan's Boys' Home
Boys Town, NE 68010

ISBN 1-889322-59-8

The Boys Town Press is the publishing division of Girls and Boys Town, the original Father Flanagan's Boys' Home.

Publisher's Cataloging in Publication

Buddenberg, Laura J.

    Who's raising your child? : battling the marketers for your child's heart and soul / by Laura J. Buddenberg and Kathleen M. McGee. -- 1st ed. -- Boys Town, NE : Boys Town Press, 2004.

    p. ; cm.

    ISBN: 1-889322-59-8

    1. Child consumers. 2. Child rearing. 3. Child psychology. 4. Consumption (Economics) 5. Target marketing. 6. Consumer protection. I. McGee, Kathleen M. II. Title.

HQ772 .B83 2004
649.1--dc22   0402

10 9 8 7 6 5 4 3 2 1

Who's RAISING your Child?

Battling the Marketers for Your Child's Heart and Soul

by

Laura J.Buddenberg & Kathleen M. McGee

BOYS
TOWN
PRESS

BOYS TOWN, NEBRASKA

Also from the Boys Town Press

Common Sense Parenting®
Common Sense Parenting of Toddlers and Preschoolers
Common Sense Parenting Learn-at-Home Video or DVD Kit
Parenting to Build Character in Your Teen
Angry Kids, Frustrated Parents
Dealing with Your Kids' 7 Biggest Troubles
Parents and Kids Talking About School Violence
Practical Tools for Foster Parents
Safe and Effective Secondary Schools
Teaching Social Skills to Youth
The Well-Managed Classroom
Unmasking Sexual Con Games
The Ongoing Journey
Journey of Faith
Journey of Hope
Journey of Love

For Adolescents

Boundaries: A Guide for Teens
A Good Friend
Who's in the Mirror?
What's Right for Me?

For a free Boys Town Press catalog, call 1-800-282-6657
Visit our web site at www.girlsandboystown.org/btpress

Girls and Boys Town National Hotline
1-800-448-3000
Parents and kids can call toll-free, anytime, with any problem.

Table of Contents

Who's Raising Your Child?

As 4-year-old Jake excitedly opened his birthday gifts, Spider-Man action figures and Incredible Hulk-related merchandise tumbled out. Then, a box revealed a toy sailboat, no logo or brand name in sight. "I don't like this one," said Jake as he put it down on the floor and reached for the next wrapped package.

• • •

In an Associated Press story on the escalating cost of high school prom nights, Raquel, a Connecticut teen, stated that "her dress cost $250; her shoes were $100; and there was $60 for a bottle of Christian Dior's J'adore, her favorite perfume. A trip to the beauty salon will cost $70, the limo is $50 a person, and it will cost $90 just to get in the door." But, Raquel said, "It's total-

ly worth it! How can you put a price tag on a lifetime of memories?"

• • •

In June 2003, six of the top 20 songs on Billboard's *singles chart had one or more product references to brands such as Mercedes, Bacardi, and Timberland, according to the Americanbrandstand.com Web site. Lucian James, founder of a brand strategy company, told MTV.com, "Hip hop is about the here and now, whereas rock and pop songs tend to be more about eternal themes of love and hate. A lot of current culture is about the things we want and own."[1]*

• • •

Sadly, it's true: *"A lot of current culture is about the things we want and own."* When preschoolers reject toys because they have no recognizable brand, when teens believe that memories of a special dance get better when they come with higher price tags, when marketing messages invade every aspect of children's lives, it's time for parents to ask, "Who's raising my child?" Is it the marketers and advertisers who tell your child that happiness is buying things, using them up, throwing them away, and then consuming even more? Or is it you, the parent, who wants to see your child find happiness by caring about, sharing with, and loving other people?

In 2001, the Motherhood Project of the Institute for American Values issued a statement to advertisers called "Watch Out for Our Children." In that statement, they wrote, "We are at a critical turn, with the very idea of childhood under attack, and with it the idea of mother-hood. ... More and more, the culture seems to teach that a good life is a materially successful life, and that a primary goal of life is to garner material possessions. According to this contemporary view of childhood, childhood is to be gotten on with as quickly as possible. In this view, what our children need most is help in promoting their cognitive development, and their ability to succeed at school and at work in order to get the material possessions they want.

"We reject this shallow, harmful, dehumanizing way of looking at childhood. It focuses almost exclusively on the material success of children and neglects the development of character. ... We know that in order to protect our children from the threats of the money world, *we* must change."[2]

That's what we'd like you, as a parent, to consider as you read this book. What impact is our hyper-commercialized society having on your child? Is your family immersed in the culture of consumption? What can *you* do to reclaim your child from the grip of advertisers?

What Kids Want

Marketers are very good at their jobs. Just look at the results. In 2002, kids from age 8 and up spent or influenced others to spend an estimated $500 billion on consumer products. Marketers spend lots of time and money on sophisticated research that tells them how to sell effectively to kids. They know that kids want to be cool and popular with their peers. They understand that kids worry that they won't fit in, that they fear being dismissed as "dorks," "nerds," or "geeks" if they differ in any way from the popular crowd with the latest clothes, fads, and music. Working on these desires and insecurities, marketers follow a simple but effective strategy to persuade kids that buying their products will meet all those needs. We'll look at that strategy in detail in the next chapter.

As parents, we need to consider whether that underlying message of marketers – *buying things will meet your needs and make you happy* – is one we want our children to believe. It's so easy for us, as adults, to fall into the same trap. How often have you thought that buying the latest model car, owning the slickest electronic gizmo, stocking your freezer with dinosaur-shaped chicken nuggets, or putting a TV set in every bedroom will solve some problem and make you and your kids happier? Is this really what you want your children to learn? It's a very self-centered, selfish approach to life.

Let's look at the example of our teen preparing for prom night. What do you think will best help her "make a lifetime of memories" – an expensive dress, shoes, and hairstyle or good friendship and relationship skills that will lead to talking, laughing, and sharing good times with her classmates at the dance? Kids are more than just consumers or objects with cash. We hope that the message you want to give your children is this: *Good relationships with friends and family will make you happy.*

The good news is that although we may disagree with the content of the message marketers give our kids, there's nothing wrong with their strategy in getting it to children and teens. In fact, if it's so effective at reaching kids, we should use it ourselves! And that's another reason for this book – to show parents how to meet kids' needs to have friends and "fit in" by teaching them to care less about things and more about other people. We'll talk about this in the next chapter and then return in detail to what parents can do in later chapters.

Marketing and Media Messages

You may be from a generation that remembers when brand names were displayed only on labels *inside* your clothing or when your favorite rock star refused to allow his music to be used in TV commercials because that was "selling out." Obviously, the world is a lot different now, but are you fully aware of the extent to which consumerism has seeped into every aspect of life? Until the early 1990s, marketers directed most of their advertising pitches to baby boomers who still dominated the market because of their sheer numbers. In 1992, two things happened: For the first time since 1975, the number of teenagers in the U.S. increased. And, according to Naomi Klein, author of *No Logo,* marketers noticed that the industries that had maintained or jumped in sales through the recession were those that catered to children, teens, and young adults – soft drinks, fast food, sneakers, and beer.

"Gradually," Klein writes, "an idea began to dawn on many in the manufacturing sector and entertainment industries: maybe their sales were slumping not because consumers were 'brand-blind,' but because their companies had their eyes fixed on the wrong demographic prize. This was not a time for selling Tide and Snuggle to housewives – it was a time for beaming MTV, Nike, Hilfiger, Microsoft, Netscape and Wired to global teens and their overgrown imitators. Their parents might have gone bargain basement, but kids, it turned out, were still willing to pay up to fit in. Through this process, peer pressure emerged as a powerful market force, making the keep-up-with-the-Joneses consumerism of their suburban parents pale by comparison."[3]

Neil Howe and William Strauss, authors of a book about the generation born in the 1980s and 1990s, call these "Millennials" a "consumer behemoth, riding atop a new youth economy of astounding scale and extravagance."[4] Fifty-seven million Americans aged 8 to 21 earn about $211 billion annually, spending all but $39 billion of it, according to research firm Harris Interactive. And the opinions of these Millennials influence many more billions of dollars in purchases made by adults.

As a result, our kids are now the most marketed-to generation ever, and we need to fully understand this phenomenon in order to deal with it. So we'll investigate the hyper-commercialized world of tykes (birth to age 7), tweens (8- to 12-year-olds), and teenagers. For each age group, we'll have some suggestions on what parents can do to limit the effects of marketing on children.

It used to be that there was a protected environment for children and common agreement about what was good and bad for kids. The media that carried marketing messages to kids clearly distinguished between child and adult content. For example, the Federal Communications Commission ensured that television executives created appropriate programs for children, and networks set aside an hour each evening for family shows where sexual content and violence were banned. Now with the advent of cable television, broadcasters and marketers pretty much concede, "the family hour doesn't really exist any more."[5]

Today, the dividing line between adult and child content in the media is increasingly blurred:

- Producers of movies that carry PG-13 ratings sign licensing agreements for action figures and other toys that are marketed to toddlers.

- Teen clothing retailers such as Abercrombie and Fitch feature nudity and sexual content in their catalogs.

- Britney Spears, a former Mouseketeer with a huge following of preteen female fans, appears on a music awards show in virtually see-through clothing.

- Hip-hop artists produce videos laced with profanity and sexualized violence, and filled with product brand references not only to automobiles and shoes but also to liquor.

While some marketers try to distance themselves from the raciest, raunchiest, and most violent content, many others advertise on and support such media content because it has proven successful for them – it sells their product.

In our work with parents, we've noticed that a substantial number of them are truly shocked by the examples we show them of what's out there in the media and available to their children. So, even if you think you're aware of everything your child is watching, reading, and listening to, read Chapters 9 and 10. Often, when the media are criticized, performers, producers, and marketers respond, "It's the parent's job, not ours, to monitor what kids are watching." You can't do a good job of monitoring unless you're aware of the total environment. These chapters will give you a good picture of what you're up against. In Chapter 11, we'll have suggestions on how to deal with the toxic marketing and media environment that threatens your kids.

Who We Are

As authors of this book, we are speaking as professionals and parents who face these issues daily – Laura has two teenaged daughters, and Kathie is the mother of a toddler. Together, we have taught and worked with troubled children and teens at Girls and Boys Town for more than 20 years. As professional trainers, we have presented workshops on relationships, the media, and sexual harassment and abuse to children and their parents in schools and churches across the country. Our work draws directly on Girls and Boys Town's many years of experience in serving children and families through programs such as schools, residential group homes, emergency shelters, foster care, parent training, and a national crisis hotline.

Girls and Boys Town wants to sell something, too. We're marketing good character, values, and good relationships between parents and kids. We want children to grow up in a world that protects them. We want kids to learn how to make good decisions, take responsibility (and accept the consequences) for their actions, learn right from wrong, and build strong, healthy relationships. That's not an easy task in this consumer society where the acquisition of things has become so important. But we believe it is the right thing to do. We hope you do, too. And we hope the information and suggestions in this book help you raise a child with strength of character and the skills to respect and care about other people.

How Marketers
Sell to Kids

Persuaders of all kinds – from prophets to dictators, political candidates to marketers – use basically the same strategy to convince their audience to believe, vote for, or buy what they're advocating. The *content* of the persuader's message can be good or bad, but the *strategy* itself is neutral and powerful. Let's look at how the strategy can be used for a variety of messages. Susan B. Anthony's campaign for women's suffrage is an example of positive persuasion; an example of persuasion with evil purpose is Adolf Hitler who persuaded others to join his mission of European domination and annihilation of the Jews.

First, the persuader issues a warning, identifies an enemy, points to a problem, or induces a fear. From

1845 to her death in 1906, Susan B. Anthony ignored opposition and abuse as she campaigned first against slavery and then the denial of educational opportunities, labor protection, and equal pay for equal work for women and ex-slaves. Adolf Hitler and his Minister of Propaganda Joseph Goebbels told the German people they had been sold out and weakened by the Treaty of Versailles at the conclusion of World War I and betrayed by the Jews living among them.

Secondly, the persuader tells people that their circumstances could be much better. Anthony believed that conditions for women would improve when they had the right to vote. The Nazis promised Germans that they could be powerful, superior, and a great nation again.

Finally, persuaders urge their audience, "Follow us, we'll show you how to get what you want." In 1862, Anthony and Elizabeth Cady Stanton formed the American Equal Rights Association and promoted women's suffrage by publishing a newspaper, conducting speaking tours and petition drives, and appearing before every Congress from 1869 to 1906. Hitler convinced many Germans to participate in his attempt to eliminate the Jews and conquer the rest of Europe.

As you can see, the strategy of persuasion can be potent and powerful in many arenas. Marketers use a version of the same strategy when selling to children. Here's what their messages tell kids:

- "You're not cool."
- "You need to be cool."
- "Follow us, we'll show you how to be cool."

'You're Not Cool'

The first thing a lot of advertising aimed at teens does is make them feel bad about themselves. How many real teens are as skinny, beautiful, clear skinned, hip, and even sexy looking as the young models who populate the ads in magazines and on television? It can be pretty alluring for teens to believe the suggestion that buying whatever product the gorgeous celebrity or fabulously wealthy athlete is endorsing will give them a bit of that "good life" too. Younger kids see a parade of enticing things – snack foods, soft drinks, toys, computer games – and feel deprived if they don't have them.

It is the (unspoken) goal of advertising to convince kids to be perpetually unhappy. Marketers show children that there's something lacking in their lives, in their looks, in their possessions. And, if they're unhappy, kids will search for a way to become happy.

'You Need to Be Cool'

There's tremendous pressure on kids, particularly teens, to conform, fit in, and keep up with their peers.

17% of schoolchildren said their **favorite** word was "**cool**." Their next favorite words were "wicked," "bling-bling" (flashy jewelry), "mint" (having money), "groovy," and "kerch-ing" (money).

Source: Survey of 20,000 children by Penguin Books, 2003

Marketers know this, and use this "fear factor" – the fear of being "out of it," a dork, a geek, a nerd – as the underlying message of much advertising to kids. It's why even a 4-year-old turns up his nose at a toy because it's not connected to a "cool" brand. Or why your teen has to have only the most expensive athletic shoes endorsed by the latest NBA superstar and no other.

U.S. Advertising Expenditures

1980 $106 Billion

2001 $230 Billion

Source: McCann-Erickson U.S. Advertising Volume Reports

"Advertising at its best is making people feel that without their product, you're a loser," Nancy Shalek, former advertising agency president, told the *Los Angeles Times*. "Kids are very sensitive to that. If you tell them to buy something, they are resistant. But if you tell them they'll be a dork if they don't, you've got their attention. You open up emotional vulnerabilities and it's very easy to do with kids because they're emotionally vulnerable."[1]

Creating even more pressure is the increasing speed at which things move from cool to "out of it." In *USA Today*, Jon Hein, creator of Jumptheshark.com which tracks when hot trends go cold, says, "The way culture is these days, everything is so five minutes ago. There's a lot more available to us in a much shorter period of time. So these cycles keep churning and churning."[2] So kids keep thinking that the next purchase of the latest craze merchandise is just what they need to be cool.

'Follow Us'

Of course, the final step of the strategy is for marketers to promise that they can supply whatever product kids need – what to wear, what to eat or drink, which music to listen to, what to apply to their face – for them to be "cool." By the time this step is reached, they've changed kids' wants into needs. Clothing is a basic need. A hip-hugging, bell-bottomed pair of jeans is a want manufactured into a need by designers, retailers, and marketers. Food is a need. Green ketchup and cartoon character cookies are wants that advertising convinces kids are needs. Most parents are familiar with situations like these: a teen who says she'll just "die" without a pair of those jeans or a child who's nagging turns trips to the grocery store into torture. These kids (and, unfortunately, many parents) have been convinced by marketers that these products are necessary for their happiness.

Almost half of all parents admit that their kids would rather go to a **shopping mall** than go hiking in the woods for a family outing.

Source: Center for a New American Dream Poll, July 1999

This three-step marketing strategy, while very smart and successful, has some unhappy consequences for children. By their very nature, advertising messages encourage kids to be:

- self-centered.

- impatient.
- greedy.

What's in It for Me?

"Obey your thirst."
"You deserve a break today."
"Just do it."
"Have it your way."

The marketing slogans seem clever and harmless, but the underlying message is not: "What's important is how this will benefit me." Kids learn that self-indulgence is a good thing. Material possessions will build their self-esteem, make them feel good, and get them friends. Their identity and social status are defined by what and how much they own.

Children who use the **most media** tend to be the **least contented,** according to a 1999 Kaiser Family Foundation study.

Kids who buy into this message can become selfish and spoiled. On a societal level, it broadens the chasm between kids who can afford (or whose parents can afford) to buy what they want and the kids who can't. Some kids are so convinced of their "right" to own the things they desire, they see nothing wrong with shoplifting or stealing to get them. On the horrific end of this continuum are a few kids who have actually injured or murdered another child for nothing more than a pair of brand-name shoes.

I Want It Now!

Many kids today are hooked on instant gratification. They want things *now*. Marketers are happy to cultivate that "fast-food" buying impulse. Professional marketers have produced industry articles such as "The Nag Factor" and "The Art of Fine Whining" that instruct advertisers on how to manipulate kids into demanding their products from parents. And parents get suckered into the frenzy. Remember the store stampedes for Cabbage Patch dolls, Tickle-Me Elmo, and Beanie Babies in years past? When parents do take action to limit the "I want it now" behavior of their kids, such as avoiding the cookie and candy aisles in the grocery store, marketers strike back. Paco Underhill, author of *Why We Buy: The Science of Shopping,* writes that to counter that "alarming trend," one of his clients, a cookie manufacturer, "began securing strategic adjacencies – with appropriate aisle partners (cookies on one side of the aisle and baby food on the other, for example ...)."[3]

Marketers use clever tactics with teens as well. "Advertisers ... like to play on teen desires to be in the

65% of 200 marketing professionals responding to a survey said marketers do only a "**poor**" or "**fair**" job in marketing responsibly to children.

Source: Reveries Online Magazine,
http://reveries.com/reverb/research/coolforkids/index.html

✔

know and have the latest exclusive gear," according to *The New York Times Upfront* magazine. "When Heelys, the sneakers that can roll like skates, were first introduced, the company made sure they were hard to find by releasing just a few at a time to stores. Only after a teen feeding frenzy began did the company pack the stores with product. Result: big sales."[4]

I Want More!

From an early age, kids are taught to be consumers. Studies have shown that kids are bombarded with as many as 3,000 advertising messages per day. By age 18, an average teen will have seen or heard, either directly or indirectly, 10 million advertising messages. James McNeal, author of *The Kids Market,* says children ages 5 to 12 make about 15 requests for products during a typical shopping trip with their parents, five requests for products a day at home, and about 10 requests a day while on vacation. This amounts to about 3,000 requests per year.[5]

Kids often tell Mom and Dad what to buy for themselves and the family – what clothes are "in," what cars

In an art/essay contest for children, "What Do Kids Really Want that Money Can't Buy," the most common answers were "love," "happiness," "peace on earth," and "friends."

Source: Center for a New American Dream, www.newdream.org

are cool, what new electronic device is the best. One parent told us that his 3-year-old advised him to buy a Dodge pickup truck. Why? "'Cause it's Ram-tough, Dad."

In some families, parents spend or hand out "guilt money" in order to make up for the time they aren't spending with their kids. Other parents want children to have things that they couldn't afford to have when they were young. When parents do say "no," it can set up a wearying tug-of-war between parents and kids about money.

Many teens, in a developmental stage where they are insecure and searching for their own identity, turn to *things* to define themselves. What most fail to recognize is that acquiring the latest thing rarely brings a lasting happiness. When they become bored with that particular item, the desired result isn't achieved, or the trendy move on to some new fad, teens are left wanting still more. Buying becomes an addiction just like smoking or drinking. They need more and more to feel good, to get a "high."

What Parents Want for Kids

Self-centered.

Impatient.

Greedy.

These are what advertising and marketing teach children to be, because they want kids to become good consumers. The evidence suggests that they've succeeded all too well. Kids today are more affluent and spend more money on a wider array of merchandise than ever before. Dr. Allen Kanner, a clinical child psychologist in Berkeley, California, says the children he sees, whether they are from the inner city or wealthy suburbs, share one thing in common: a growing, even insatiable, desire for material goods. "In my practice I see kids becoming incredibly consumerist," said Kanner. "The most stark example is when I ask them what they want to do when they grow up. They all say they want to make money. When they talk about their friends, they talk about the clothes they wear, the designer labels they wear, not the person's human qualities."[6]

"When children make **requests** for things from the supermarket, slightly over **90%** are by **brand** name."

Source: James McNeal, "The Kids Market: Myths and Realities," 1999, Paramount Market Publishing

Another psychologist, Dr. Tim Kassell of Knox College in Galesburg, Illinois, studies materialism. He says that people who are highly focused on materialistic values report they are less satisfied with life, seem less happy, have a higher incidence of unsatisfactory interpersonal relationships, are more prone to drug and alcohol abuse, and contribute less to their community.[7]

What we also see here at Girls and Boys Town and among the kids we meet elsewhere is that many children today are lonely. They are surrounded by possessions, but they don't have enough warm, loving, and nurturing relationships with people.

Many kids lack the basic social skills needed to foster healthy friendships because they spend so much time interacting with "things." Watching television, playing video games, surfing the Net, even participating in online chat rooms – none of it involves face-to-face interaction that requires a whole range of interpersonal skills. A lot of technology, such as portable CD players, headphones, and handheld Gameboys, helps kids block out the social world around them. Some kids are just lost when it comes to holding a conversation with an adult or knowing how to approach a new kid in the neighborhood.

We believe that this is not what most parents want for their children. Think about the kind of person you'd like your child to be or become. We hope you want your child to be:

- Someone who genuinely cares about other people, values others for who they are and not what they look like or own, and shows love for family and friends.

- Someone who demonstrates responsibility and can set and work toward long-term goals.

- Someone who is willing to share with and give to others.

Children don't just naturally acquire these virtues. They need to be taught, primarily by parents. And with so much of the popular culture working against parents, it can be a tough task. If kids get 3,000 messages per day urging them to buy more things, how do you recapture their attention and teach them to focus on people-oriented goals?

What Parents Can Do

Parents, first of all, can learn from the marketers' success. Kids are great consumers because they've been convinced by advertisers that "stuff" will get kids what they want – popularity, a cool look, a way to feel good. We think parents can use the same three-step sales strategy that marketers use, but with a different message and for a very different purpose.

First, parents should acknowledge that children's needs are important. Kids need to have friends and feel that they fit in. They need to find their own unique identity and gradually accept responsibility and gain independence as they grow. Kids should know that you see those as valid goals for them, too.

Second, parents need to reassure kids that they can be successful at reaching those goals. The route to those

Major Sources of Income for Children Ages 4-12

Allowances	45%
Household Work	21%
Gifts from Parents	16%
Work Outside the Home	10%
Gifts from Others	8%

Source: James McNeal, "The Kids Market: Myths and Realities," 1999, Paramount Market Publishing

goals, however, will not be the one marketers have mapped out for them. Parents can show children that their path to happiness depends on relationships with other people and not with the acquisition of things.

And finally, parents can say, "Follow us, we'll teach you the skills you need to make friends, earn the respect of others, and be happy in life." In other words, parents need to sell pro-social behavior as the "product" that will get their kids the same payoffs the marketers promise – friendship, happiness, and success. And, unlike the marketers' products, what you are "selling" your kids will never be used up, go out of style, or fail to deliver on its promise! You will be teaching them skills that are useful for a lifetime.

We're not implying this will be easy. Marketing messages are everywhere, and the violent, sexual content of the media that carry the messages can be damaging to kids as well. You will have to make rules, enforce consequences, teach skills, and be a good role model. You will need to set an example, probably by changing at least some of your own media habits and purchasing decisions. It will be hard work, but that's the definition of parenting, isn't it?

We urge you to think of the payoff, however, both for your child and you. Kids may grump and groan at rules and restrictions, but ultimately they know that this means you love them and care about what happens to them. Putting relationships first in your family and de-emphasizing the quest for material possessions benefits everyone at home. Your child gets the powerful message that we're supposed to use things and love people, not love things and use people. That's a message our kids need to understand.

3

Tykes and Television

More and more parents are naming their children after brand-name products. According to the 2000 census, there were six American children named Timberland, 49 Canons, 11 Bentleys, five Jaguars, and one Xerox.

● ● ●

Marketing experts admit their goal is "to become part of the fabric of (children's) lives ...," "to own (children) younger and younger and younger ...," and to "nurture kids as future consumers."[1] The food and beverage industries spend an estimated $13 billion on marketing that targets children.[2] There's a lot of cash on the line. MarketResearch.com states that kids ages 4 to

12 spent more than $40 billion in 2002 and that their direct buying power is expected to climb to more than $51.8 billion by 2006.[3]

In response, marketing firms, market research companies, and publications that exclusively focus on selling to children and teens have proliferated. Annual "summits" that strategize how to market to kids draw hundreds of participants from the broadcasting and cable networks, entertainment industry, publishers, and toy and food companies. This is a typical session on one such summit agenda: "Programmers from top kids' broadcasters map out their channel strategies, providing essential info on their audience, ratings, buying needs, marketing, on-air branding, pitching preferences and burgeoning kids programming trends."[4]

The evidence shows the marketers have been spectacularly successful:

- In one poll of parents, 20 percent said their kids by age 3, before they could read, began asking for brand-name products.[5]

- Almost half of the parents said that kids were asking for branded products by age 5.[6]

- A Stanford University study found that one 30-second commercial could influence brand choices of children as young as 2.[7]

As a result, companies with adult product lines have found ways to promote their brand to children, hoping to establish a loyalty that kids will carry with them into adulthood. For example, Home Depot sells toy tools, clothing retailer Tommy Hilfiger markets dolls dressed in his designer-label togs, and Harley-Davidson has branded baby clothes and toy motorbikes. Even luxury retailers like Coach, Polo Ralph Lauren, Burberry, and Tiffany are creating products to extend their brands into the kids market. "The best way to do it is to get (kids) involved – wearing the clothes, feeling the charisma, emulating the values seen in magazines, on runways, on parents – as early as possible," says Arnold Aronson, a marketing strategist.[8] The payoff can be big: A lifetime customer can be worth $100,000 to a retailer, according to *American Demographics.*

Children influence an estimated 72% of family food and beverage purchases.

Source: American Demographics, December 1999

Marketers are even signing up toddlers to promote their products. *USA Today* reports that Reebok is building a marketing campaign around a 3 1/2-year-old "basketball sharpshooter." The ads will feature home movies of the tyke at 21 months old in diapers shooting at a kiddie hoop.[9] No one knows whether or not the college trust being set up to pay the youngster's family will make him ineligible to play high school and college basketball in the future.

Children can also be heavily influenced by advertising that is intended for adults. For example, more than 90 percent of 6-year-olds in some studies were able to match the Joe Camel cartoon image with pictures of a cigarette. That rivals kids' recognition of Mickey Mouse. In contrast, only 67 percent of adults recognized Joe Camel.[10]

Television Advertising

Marketing reaches children 7 years of age and younger primarily through television. "In 1998," writes marketing critic and author Robert McChesney, "broadcasters even began targeting one-year-olds to get a toehold on the youth market. In a moment of candor, one Time Warner children's television executive conceded that 'there's something vaguely evil' about programming to kids that young. Nobody knows what the effects of this unprecedented commercial indoctrination of children will be down the road. The only thing we know for sure is that the people responsible don't care."[11]

There is research that advertising affects choices made by children as young as 2. One study showed two groups of Head Start children (ages 2-6) a half-hour cartoon program; one group saw it uninterrupted, the other saw ads for candy, cereal, doughnuts, toys, etc., interspersed in the program. The children were then asked to select their preferences when given choices between advertised and non-advertised but similar products. In most cases, the children who viewed the ads overwhelmingly selected the advertised products – even when the advertised products were new to them and placed next to a familiar product – while the kids who saw no ads did not.[12]

Some governments have tried to protect children from the barrage of advertising.

- In Sweden and Norway, no ads are allowed on programs intended for children under the age of 12.

- Greece prohibits toy advertising on television during certain hours.

- Ads are banned from late afternoon TV in Ireland.[13]

In the U.S., the 1990 Children's Television Act limited advertising time but not what can be advertised. The Act restricts commercial time on programs primarily produced for those 12 and younger to 10.5 or 12 minutes per hour depending on the day. Those minutes, however, can still pack quite a marketing wallop. We randomly selected one half-hour program running on the WB network's "Kids Saturday Morning" lineup. *Thirty* commercials or promos – everything from fast food and high-tech toys to PG-13 movies and a belching contest – ran in two long sequences during this

36% of children 6 and younger have TVs in their bedrooms.

68% of children under 2 are in front of a screen for more than two hours a day.

Source: Kaiser Family Foundation and Children's Digital Media Center Report, October 2003

30-minute show. (See the end of this chapter for a complete rundown of the ads.)

Despite the limits, children still see about 40,000 televised commercials each year. And the two things sold most to them on TV are toys and food.[14]

Food Ads and Kids

Years ago, a parent's toughest food battle was getting Johnny to eat his vegetables. Now, kids are challenging parents over the colors, shapes, and brands of everything they eat, from breakfast cereal to cookies. This is not news to parents familiar with the nagging, whining, and tantrums employed by kids in the grocery store and at the dinner table. We know of one child who refused to eat the good old American-staple hamburger unless it came from McDonald's.

A U.S. Department of Agriculture study found that most of the billions of dollars spent on food advertising in this county is focused on highly processed, highly packaged foods – confectioneries, convenience foods, snacks, and soft drinks that are high in sugar and/or fat.[15] "The market for packaged foods like ketchup, mustard and frozen goods is a mature market," Andrew

According to marketing industry studies, a person's brand loyalty may begin as early as age 2.

Source: "Brand Aware," Children's Business, June 2000

Lazar, analyst with Lehman Brothers, told CNN/Money. "Therefore companies need to continually innovate. Most food manufacturers also focus heavily on kids because of their potential to create incremental sales for a company's products."[16]

Consumer advocate Peggy Charren says, "We've found that 98 percent of the food advertising is for products children don't have to eat, nonnutritive things. Now in fact they are designing foods that would never be on the market if it were not for television and its ability to sell them."[17] Increasingly, health experts point to this flood of "junk food" advertising as contributing to the rising rate of childhood obesity. (According to a report from the National Institutes of Health, the rate of obesity in kids increased two-and-a-half times between 1980 and 2000.)

At times, the only good news for parents in this arena seems to be the occasional missteps taken by food marketers. H.J. Heinz, riding high on the success of its green, purple, and pink ketchups, pulled its "Funky Fries" from grocery store shelves when even kids refused to demand its chocolate-flavored French fries. (We can only imagine the legions of parents heaving sighs of relief!)

Additionally, a few food marketers are pulling back from marketing to kids in the wake of the uproar over obesity and threatened lawsuits. Coke now has a policy prohibiting its marketers from aiming ads for any of its beverages, including bottled water and fruit juices, as well as any of its trademarked merchandise such as toys, at children under 12. (The policy does not prohibit Coke's beverages from being sold in school vending machines or putting Coke signs on athletic field scoreboards.)[18]

Children's Programming

One of the arguments for advocating a ban on television advertising aimed at kids is that very young children don't know the difference between ads and programming. But the impact of banning or limiting advertising during children's programs might be minimal because today there is so much product placement *within* the shows. Many programs are created solely for their marketing potential and are little more than one long commercial. One parent told us how "The Mighty Morphin Power Rangers" dominate his young son's life: "He makes the same sounds they do; he plays with the same toys; he knows each episode; he knows each kick and punch. The Rangers are his role models. I'm not. And it scares me. Especially because I let it happen."

Marketing has become "the tail that wags the dog," even in what used to be the realm of commercial-free educational television on the Public Broadcasting System (PBS). The majority of money for PBS programming used to come from the public sector, our taxes, and other governmental funding. Now, because of budget cuts at the federal level, public broadcasting has to find other ways to foot the bill, including corporate sponsorship and marketing and licensing deals.

PBS's popular program "Sesame Street" has provided kids with positive, educational, and moral messages

"When it comes to targeting kid consumers, we at General Mills follow the Proctor and Gamble model of **'cradle to grave.'** ... We believe in getting them early and having them for life."

Source: Wayne Chilicki, quoted in Mothering Magazine, No. 97 (Nov./Dec.)

for more than 30 years. Studies have proven that kids who regularly watch "Sesame Street" do better in school, especially in math and science. But the program has also spawned a huge merchandising empire, with Kermit the Frog, Miss Piggy, Bert and Ernie, Big Bird, and Grover beckoning kids from toys, lunch boxes, books, movies, and more. The licensing money keeps a show that endorses healthy values for kids on the air, but at a price, as millions of toddlers "must have" all things Bert and Ernie.

Other programs that can't pay that price because they have few merchandising opportunities may disappear. The innovative, Emmy Award-winning "Reading Rainbow" premiered in 1983 to introduce children to the joys of books and reading. In the summer of 2003, "Reading Rainbow" faced cancellation due to lack of funding and licensing deals. It has no action figures, no lunch boxes, and no clothing line. Executive producer and host LeVar Burton desperately sought private funding to keep the program on the air.

On commercial television, it used to be that only the advertising time within children's programming was used to sell products. Now, programs themselves are often created *around* a marketing or merchandising concept. The real money is made from the toy and food licensing deals that are signed before the show ever hits the airwaves.

Finally, we know that kids watch much more than what's labeled as "children's programming" and are often exposed to advertising that is intended for adults. For example, a young child watching Sunday afternoon football with his Dad could see commercials for adult products like beer that contain cursing, sexual suggestiveness, violence, and crude behavior. The ads are not only selling products that are inappropriate for children, but are also modeling inappropriate behavior for kids.

Cross-Marketing

Marketing tie-ins aimed at kids are everywhere. When a new cartoon-character movie is produced, images of the super hero pop up on cereal boxes and frozen waffle packages. Some kids won't go to bed unless they're wearing their Spider-Man pajamas. These cross-marketing campaigns are successful even when the children who are targeted with this merchandise are *too young* to see the original PG-13 rated movie. The first movie to have a mass marketing campaign of licensed spin-off merchandise was "Star Wars" in 1977. The Toy Industry Association estimates that sales of licensed toys, figures, and other products from that film have earned $2.5 billion.[19]

For G-rated movies, toys are the hottest movie-related merchandise. The big 2003 summer movie for kids, "Finding Nemo," had fish-shaped stuffed animals, plastic swimming toys, T-shirts, and stickers on store shelves before the film was in theaters. Retailers also expect toy sales from big movies to carry into the Christmas season and then get another boost when the movie is released on videotape or DVD.[20]

> **$13 billion was spent in 2002 to market food and drinks to American children.**
>
> *Source: New York University Department of Nutrition and Food Studies Report*

Toy manufacturers now also create toys that advertise food. For example, Susan Linn and Diane E. Levin write in *The Christian Science Monitor,* "Mattel now produces a McDonald's Barbie 'fun time play set.' The box, adorned with the enticement, 'Lots of yummy food,' contains miniature French fries, Big Macs, and other high-calorie delights – including a Sprite soft drink machine. Hasbro offers a McDonald's Play-Doh set with molds for burgers, buns, and machines for churning out shakes and soft-serve ice cream."[21]

In return, the fast-food industry uses popular toys or merchandise tied to movies and TV shows to lure families to the drive-through lanes. This prompts kids to nag Mom or Dad to keep returning until all four (or five or six!) action figures or toys have been collected. When miniature Beanie Babies were offered as prizes with fast-food meals, there were traffic jams at many franchises and reports at others of people buying the meals and immediately throwing the food away because they were only interested in the toy! During the movie "Rugrats Go Wild," numbers appeared occasionally in the corner of the screen. Kids were supposed to scratch and sniff the same number on a card that could only be obtained by visiting Burger King.

The world of children's books has been invaded by snack foods. Kids can learn to count (and presumably crave these sugary treats) by reading *Skittles Riddles Math, The Cheerio's Counting Book,* and *The Hershey's Kisses Addition Book.* The back cover of *The Oreo Cookie Counting Book* promises that "(c)hildren will love to count down as ten little OREOs are dunked, nibbled and stacked one by one ... until there are none!"

Clifford the Big Red Dog, a classic children's book for 40 years, has now become a multimedia marketing juggernaut. In 2002, *Clifford's* licensing revenue for its TV cartoon show and other products was $350 million. Its publisher, Scholastic Books, has even bigger plans for the lovable pet. These include a TV spinoff on PBS called "Clifford's Puppy Days," a Fisher-Price touch-and-read book, a Hasbro Play-Doh set, a commercial playground set, a home play swing set, a live touring show, and a feature-length animated movie. In addition, Lipton Soup will feature Clifford giveaways and activity sets with its Soup

Secrets line, and Bounty will offer Clifford paper towels.[22]

Marketers have still other ploys to target children. Kids are offered "free issues" of comic books if they fill out the information card placed on the back of packaged toys. This information, of course, is then placed in a database. Other offers, promotions, and sales pitches then begin arriving in the mail. Kids are also encouraged to join clubs that offer fun and discounts for the kids, but ultimately promote products for corporations.

Marketing's Effects on Toddlers

What can the consequences be for young children as targets of this flood of advertising and marketing messages? As researchers reported to Congress in 2003, advertising has been linked to family stress and negative values, as well as to increased violence, obesity, and eating disorders in children.

Children imitate what they see on television.

This can be a good thing if they're watching shows such as "Sesame Street" or "Mister Rogers' Neighborhood." But it can be harmful when they're watching a menu of programs and commercials heavy on violence, rude behavior, or inappropriate for their age. A 1996 National Television Violence Study found that children's programs were least likely to depict the long-term consequences of violence and portrayed violence in a humorous fashion 67 percent of the time. Look again at the list at the end of this chapter of commercials and promotions running during that typical half-hour of Saturday morning children's programming. Even though sometimes depicting the action as funny, the ads show kids belching, kicking, fighting, and "blasting" adults off into space – not exactly behavior you'd like to see your kids imitate.

Some toys, video games, and TV can diminish kids' creativity and imagination.

A 4-year-old can make a set of blocks be whatever he wants them to be, from a fort to a train to a tower to a herd of animals. With other toys, play is often "scripted" simply because of what the toy is and how it is promoted. For example, a Spider-Man action figure can only be Spider-Man. A 3-year-old explained it this way, "Spidey *has* to kill the Green Goblin 'cuz he's a bad guy. Spidey's the good guy."

Social scientists worry that TV and computer games offer up packaged plotlines, characters, and scripts, inhibiting the development of imagination. Research has found that unstructured and open-ended play, on the other hand, "helps increase concentration and attention, and gives kids the chance to socialize, express emotions and practice motor skills." Jerome and Dorothy Singer, who study children and play, "have consistently found that kids who engage in pretend play also laugh and smile more and show less aggression than kids who play less imaginatively."[23]

Advertising can use images that are unsettling for toddlers at the least and downright scary at the worst.

Monsters, demons, robots, strange creatures, and weird adults are just a few of the odd, frightening characters that inhabit the world of children's commercials.

Marketing messages and excessive TV viewing can be harmful to kids' health.

Since 1980, the rate of childhood obesity has more than doubled, and researchers suspect the marketing emphasis on high-sugar, high-fat foods is at least partially to blame.[24] When kids are glued to the tube, they are also missing out on other activities and relationships that could benefit them physically, emotionally, and socially.

Advertising encourages nagging, whiny, greedy behavior in kids.

Young children especially may have trouble with understanding concepts of delaying expectations, planning, saving, or budgeting. After all, even if Mom doesn't have cash, she's always got that magic piece of plastic that can be used to buy just about anything. And many kids learn that if they're persistent enough when they nag, Mom or Dad will eventually give in and buy them something, anything to keep them quiet! Kids may also attempt to equate parents' love with their willingness to buy them what they want. How often have you heard

something like this: "You never buy me *anything!*" or
"*Billy's* dad got *him* a Brand XYZ Super-Duper Gizmo!
Why can't *I* get one?"

With all these potential negative effects of advertising, what can parents do to eliminate or mitigate them?
The following chapter will offer some strategies for
parents to consider.

Ads on Saturday Morning TV

We randomly selected a program to watch from the
WB "Kids Saturday Morning" lineup. Here are the 30
commercials that ran in staccato sequence during two
breaks for the program in a half-hour period:

1. An upside-down kid belches, and a gruesome
   monster's face appears below him. It's an ad for
   the Burpilicious Belch-a-Thon 2003.

2. A Juicy Fruit ad depicts an older girl with a
   pack of gum as a group of younger kids scream
   "Gimme some." After a man warns about
   "moochers" wanting your gum, the girl holds a
   car door in front of her and rolls up the window. The man intones, "Whoa! Denied!"

3. A fast-paced commercial shows two boys playing with the high-tech toys, Power Megazoid
   and Lightning Megazoid.

4. An ad celebrates the brand-new television series,
   "Megaman" and "Yugis Duelin' Tips and
   Tricks Training Camp."

5. An ad promotes the WB's new "Hero-Stuffed
   Saturday."

6. An ad promotes the new show, "Teen Titans."

7. A commercial starts with a voice-over saying, "Friendships are in trouble and it's up to you to bring harmony back." The ad is for the Ham-Ham-Hamtaro game.

8. An ad announces "Sweepstakes, giveaways, and much more!"

9. In another Burpilicious Belch-a-Thon commercial, two animated characters and a boy get their burps rated on the Belch-O-Meter.

10. A fast-paced ad promotes the WB's "Zany, Insany April."

11. A WB ad shows a car smashing into a building, which signals a return to the program.

At the next break:

12. Three kids belch in another ad for the Burpilicious Belch-a-Thon.

13. In a "Star Trek"-like ad for Wendy's kids' meals, a voice-over states "This mission is not for adults because Wendy's kids' meals are just for kids." Kids take off in a spaceship and glide through a Crispy Nugget field, encountering two dorky-looking guys on a tandem bicycle. One boy says, "Unidentified Flying Adults" and "Fire!" The adults then disappear from the screen. A voice-over says, "Look to see what's inside a kids' meal. 'Hey Arnold' toys. There's one new 'Hey Arnold' toy in every kid's meal; you can collect all five. While supplies last at

participating Wendy's. Ask for alternative toy for children under 3."

14. An ad for cute and cuddly Micropets says, "Micropets are collectible. Each sold separately." This is followed by an ad for the Micropets Web site.

15. Another Burpilicious Belch-a-Thon ad shows two kids and an animated character belching. Scooby Doo pokes his head up during the ad.

16. An ad promotes "Pokemon" and "Master Quest."

17. An ad promotes the "Static Shock" program.

18. An ad for Fruit Roll-Ups shows kids shooting each other with a gooey substance.

19. Another Burpilicious Belch-a-Thon ad shows a boy belch. This is followed by ads for "Pokemon" and "Static Shock." The ad ends with a little girl belching.

20. An ad promotes Power Rangers Ninja Storm toys, Power Megazoid and Lightning Megazoid.

21. An ad promotes the WB's "Zany, Insany April."

22. An ad promotes "X-Men Evolution."

23. An ad promotes "Smallville."

24. An ad promotes the movie, "X-Men United," rated PG-13.

25. An ad promotes "Teenage Mutant Ninja Turtles."

26. An ad for the WB shows young teenagers looking cool.

27. In an ad for the "Cramp Twins" (as in intestinal cramps), a voice-over says, "The twins are as compatible as knitting and explosives." Kids are shown kicking, fighting, and pointing fingers at each other.

28. An ad promotes the new program, "Teen Titans."

29. An ad promotes the WB's "Hero-Stuffed Saturday."

30. A final ad promotes the Burpilicious Belch-a-Thon.

What Parents of
Tykes Can Do

There are things parents can do to counteract the negative effects of the marketing that's directed at very young children. Here are some strategies particularly suited for use with kids up to age 7. (Please note that *none* of them involves the spending of money!)

Set limits on your child's television time.

One of the best ways to limit the effects of TV advertising on children is simply to limit the amount of time they are allowed to watch it. Many experts recommend that preschoolers watch no more than one hour of TV daily. If children learn when they are young to develop other interests such as reading (or looking at picture books), riding a bike, or playing with toys or friends, they are more likely to continue doing so as they get older. Parents are role models for their kids here too. If you watch a lot of TV, chances are your child will also.

Help your child be selective in what he or she does watch. Turn the TV set on only to watch specific, pre-selected programs. Don't let kids just randomly turn the set on and then "surf" the channels. Needless to say, we don't think it's ever a good idea to allow a preschooler to have a television set in his or her bedroom.

Watch TV with your child.

By watching TV with your child, you not only monitor what the child is viewing, but also have the opportunity to comment on, explain, or answer questions about the advertising and program content. You can serve as a filter to help your child understand what's happening on the screen. You can help very young children distinguish between the program and the commercials, between reality and make-believe. For insight into your child's perceptions and feelings, ask your child questions about what you are viewing together. If your child is watching Sunday afternoon football with you and inappropriate advertising is aired, hit the "mute" button and distract your child with a quick game or a discussion of a favorite player or the last big play.

Teach your child to take "No" for an answer.

Nagging and whining come naturally to children! They must be taught how to accept a "No" answer calmly. Choose a quiet, neutral time to teach this skill. In other words, don't bother trying to talk this over with your child when she's sobbing in the grocery cart because you won't buy her a candy bar. When she is calm, explain to her that there will be times when she will ask for something and you will have to tell her "No." Tell her that when that happens, you want her to look at you, say "Okay, Mom," and sit or stand quietly. Have her repeat those steps back to you and then set up a "practice" situation so she can run through the steps with you. Praise her for doing this with you. You may have to remind your daughter and practice this many times, but it should ultimately lead to more cooperation and fewer tantrums when you say "No."

A few hints: Try to make practice varied and fun for your child. For example, think of "crazy" situations ("Mom, can I have broccoli for dessert?") or ask your child to come up with one. When you do have to say "No" to your child, give a short, understandable reason to your child so your answer doesn't appear arbitrary. ("Keisha, you can't have a candy bar now because we're going to eat lunch as soon as we get home.") This is *not* an invitation to a debate or argument between you and your child. Repeated requests or whining should be handled by ignoring the behavior or giving a consequence to your child for the misbehavior.

Do some "preventive teaching" before you take your child on shopping trips.

Right before you leave on a shopping excursion is a good time to remind your child of or ask him to list the rules for such trips. For example, "Sit quietly with a book or toy in the cart; don't whine or nag or ask for things that aren't on the shopping list." Occasionally, you can offer a reward for good behavior, but try not to make it the purchase of something for the child. Promise to play a game or stop at the park if he or she behaves well on the outing.

Praise your child for pro-social behavior such as sharing toys with playmates or comforting a crying friend.

You want to encourage your child to get along well with other children, to be respectful toward adults, to make friends, and to be empathetic with others. So try to catch your child doing these things! When you spot him taking turns on the swing set or quietly playing with his sister, be sure to praise him for it. Make sure you describe the behavior so your child has no doubt about what pleased you.

Teach your child simple social skills.

Showing young children how to use some basic "people" skills, such as introducing themselves, carrying on a conversation, and sharing toys, can be of great benefit to them as they grow older. When kids have good relationship skills, making friends and "fitting in" will be much easier for them, especially as teens. List and demonstrate the steps of these social skills to your child, and then help them find opportunities to practice them.

Reward your child with time and attention rather than with things.

Hugs, kisses, time spent with Mom and Dad – these are what young kids really crave. So give your child "people" rewards when he or she has earned them. Make a list of possibilities to choose from – shooting hoops with Dad, an extra bedtime story, playing a board game together, having a friend over to spend the night, etc. – so you're ready when the opportunity arises.

If you want to get your child a special toy or food item, ask him or her to do some chore or task to "earn" the treat.

Even when kids don't get an allowance or hold a job, it's important to teach them that things aren't free. They also can learn that something attained through work and effort is very satisfying. It can be a way for you to discuss how you earn and budget the money that buys food, clothing, shelter, and all the extras for your family. Let your child know that you aren't able to buy everything you might like to, that some purchases must be put off until money can be saved to make them, and that you must make responsible choices with your money.

Encourage play activities that promote creativity, thinking and problem-solving skills, and concentration.

TV watching entertains kids; it does not engage the part of the brain that thinks critically or solves problems. Teachers often remark to us how short the attention spans of kids are getting. So help your child enjoy play-time away from the frantic visual pace of television with activities such as playing with building blocks or paints that allow the child to think creatively, plan, and puzzle out difficulties.

Find ways to involve your child in volunteer or service activity.

If you contribute to a charity or volunteer your time to an organization, look for opportunities to explain to your child why you do this or have the child assist you. For example, many churches and other organizations sponsor Christmas "giving" trees with names and infor-mation about needy families. If you select a family to assist, have your child help you choose, wrap, and deliv-er the items you will donate. If your child has a sick class-mate, ask her what she would like to do to help. It can be something as simple as making and sending a get-well card or as ambitious as running a lemonade stand to raise money to help with medical expenses. Encourage your child to show empathy and caring for other people.

Using these strategies successfully when your chil-dren are young will help them develop a sound system of values that puts people first. They may still get enticed by the latest toy or snack food on the market, but you will have given them a larger framework within which to consider their desires and choices. It should make the parenting tasks coming during the preteen and teenage years somewhat easier.

5

Marketing
to Tweens

In a McGraw-Hill textbook for 11- to 13-year-olds, the math problem asks: "Will is saving his allowance to buy a pair of Nike shoes that cost $68.25. If Will earns $3.25 per week, how many weeks will Will need to save?"[1]

• • •

Debbie Travis, host of an HGTV redecorating show, says 40 percent of her fan mail comes from tweens. Companies like Martha Stewart Kids, BombayKids, and Pottery Barn Kids are marketing bedroom furniture, linens, and faux finishes directly to preteens. It's not unheard of, according to Carol Green, president of Children's Creative Marketing, for parents to spend $50,000 on a child's bedroom.[2]

• • •

"Tween girls rule!" says Buzz, *a kids marketing newsletter reporting on the 2003 Licensing Show in New York. "The number of properties targeting this demographic seems literally to have mushroomed overnight."*[3]

●　●　●

As children grow into their pre-adolescent years, they spend more time outside the home and with friends, and are exposed to a lot more media messages beyond the influence of parents. Ads plaster the facades of entire buildings; the Gap and other retailers use streetlamps to project ads onto the sidewalk at night. Sporting, cultural, and even religious events advertise their corporate sponsorships.

At school, on the Internet, and at the movies, tweens – kids ages 8 to 12 – are bombarded with advertising, both blatant and subtle. Developmentally, they are beginning their search for an identity separate from parents and family, so they are especially vulnerable to manipulative advertising that plays on their insecurities. They are anxious to "grow up," and marketers exploit this desire by targeting younger and younger audiences for products that were once considered appropriate only for teens or adults (cosmetics or "sexy" clothing styles, for example). At this age, children are increasingly influenced by their peers and less by their parents.

Marketers have put tweens under the microscope. They create "clubs" where personal information is required for registration online or through the mail. Kids earn prizes for answering surveys or participating in

When children go online:

26% agree to give details of what their parents did on the weekend.

54% are willing to tell the names of their parents' favorite stores.

66% will disclose the names of their favorite online stores.

39% tell how much monthly allowance they receive.

Source: Annenberg Public Policy Center study, University of Pennsylvania

polls. Focus groups are disguised as slumber parties where marketers judge the reaction of kids to products they receive as giveaways.

There's a compelling reason for all the research: Tweens have lots of money. In 2002, the 23 million tweens in the U.S. spent $20 billion and influenced others to spend another $200 billion. And tween spending is growing by about 15 percent a year.[4]

Tween consumers appear to be especially good at nagging their parents. In one survey, kids estimated that they asked their parents for something they had seen advertised an average of *nine times* before their parents finally gave in. But older tweens (12- to 13-year-olds) were the champion naggers – some of them admitted to asking for things *50 times*. These kids also say that even when they know their parents disapprove of certain products, they keep asking in the hopes their parents will finally say "Yes."[5]

Kids like these are made for marketers like Carter Kustera. Kustera is an artist who has created a line of trinkets with "inspirational" messages, such as "I love me" and "I'm the most beautiful person I've ever seen," that he wants to sell to kids. Kustera told *Advertising Age*: "Hey, I've got to make a living like anyone else. ... The kids market is the best market. Kids buy anything and parents buy everything for their kids."[6]

School Zone: Watch Out for Marketers

Schools were once a commercial-free haven for kids. But now many school districts, feeling the pinch of tight budgets, have found that marketers are eager to pay them in equipment or cash for access to their students. Perhaps the best-known example is Channel One, which provides free video equipment to schools in return for a 12-minute broadcast that includes two minutes of commercials. Companies pay up to $195,000 for a 30-second ad that reaches eight million students in 40 percent of this country's middle and high schools.[7]

Corporate advertising also has infiltrated schools in some surprising ways. Anti-drug, anti-violence, and anti-smoking assemblies have been staples in schools for years. Now, a teen marketing firm called 12 to 20 has figured out how to marry these cause-related gatherings with efforts to promote developing teen pop stars. The company arranges for big or growing artists like

Fabolous, Solange, Dream, and Play to go into junior and senior high schools, deliver some kind of inspirational message, and then perform for the captive audience. These tours are also sponsored by corporations like Ford Motor Co., PepsiCo, Levi Strauss & Co., and L'Oreal, which get signage in the school and distribute branded giveaways to the kids in the audience. Despite the "cause" sugar-coating, these tours have one main goal: "If you remember that Dream came to your school, and then you tell someone 'Look at the autograph I have from Dream,' they are going to remember that band for a long time," says a record company marketing executive.[8]

> Marketers spend $750 million annually selling snacks and processed food in schools.
>
> Source: The New York Times

Corporations are sponsoring competitions that feature their product and lure schools with big cash prizes. Oakdale Elementary in Frederick County, Maryland, won $10,000 from Oscar Mayer when students dressed up as dancing pieces of ham and cheese and sang the best interpretation of the company's bologna song and two other songs praising its Lunchables brand. Kids in 5,200 schools created replicas of everything from life-size cars to masterpiece paintings made of SweeTarts candies while vying for Nestle's $10,000 and $5,000 awards. Angel Soft toilet paper and Dunkin' Donuts have also run school-based contests.[9]

Here are some other examples of how advertising and brand names have invaded our educational systems:

- Coke and Pepsi are battling each other to sign exclusive contracts to place their vending machines inside schools.

- Companies like Shop Rite and Rust-Oleum have sponsored gyms and playing fields at schools in exchange for advertising rights.

- Math problems in a McGraw-Hill textbook are based on finding the total fat grams in a Burger King Whopper with cheese and the diameter of an Oreo cookie.

- A company called Cover Concepts makes millions of dollars giving away textbook covers that carry corporate advertising.

- Prego spaghetti sauce and Gushers fruit snacks send educational kits to science teachers that describe how to use their product in physics and geology demonstrations.

- ZapMe! Computers gave out computers to 1,800 schools in 45 states in return for permission to post ads on the students' screens and to collect and sell data on their Web browsing habits. (The free equipment offer was halted in 2000 following the dot.com stock market bust, and the company eventually went out of business.)

- America Online gives free software to schools that filters Internet sites and sets up school home pages and student e-mail accounts. The

AOL logo and its advertising partners are featured on screen pages.

- Many school cafeterias now offer lunches featuring Pizza Hut, Burger King, and other brand-name fast foods. School vending machines carry candy, cookies, and other snack foods.

- The Colorado Springs school district sells advertising space on the sides of its school buses and on six-foot banners hanging inside schools.

- In Chicago, The Field Trip Factory is paid to bring schoolchildren into stores and businesses on "field trips." Its clients include Petco, the Sports Authority, Pearle Vision, Giant Eagle and Dominick's grocery stores, and LaSalle Bank.

- Another company, The Mad Science Group, takes science classes that feature products from L'Oreal, Oral-B, Toys 'R' Us, and even branded Harry Potter toys to schools.

Some school administrators defend this product-marketing invasion into the classroom. They say it gives their financially strapped schools access to equipment they can't afford to purchase or allows them to offer "extras" to their students. They point out that kids are used to seeing computer screens full of advertising. Other schools claim their cafeterias have to compete with nearby fast-food chains that lure kids off campus during the lunch hour. Mike Blakeslee, deputy executive director of the National Association of Music Educators, defended the Oscar Mayer "School House Jam" contest. While they may promote a product, he told *The*

Washington Post, the "jingles are valid music. You can talk about structure, pitch, rhythmic value." The association estimates that corporations have given about $5 million to school music-education programs in the past few years, including more than $1 million from Oscar Mayer.[10]

School officials predict that corporate programs in schools are likely to increase. Dan Fuller, director of federal programs for the National School Boards Association, says that "very dire fiscal conditions in the states" plus "funding cuts in many programs, including education" will force schools to find other funding sources.[11]

Some school districts, however, have reconsidered their commercial ties. San Francisco, for example, approved policies in 1999 that forbid its teachers from using corporate-sponsored educational materials and its schools from entering into exclusive contracts with soda or snack food companies.

10% of schools are paid for allowing just **one brand** of soda on campus.

Source: National Soft Drink Association

Other school districts, as well as parents and advocacy groups such as Commercial Alert and the Center for Commercial Free Public Education, have raised questions about the proliferation of marketing messages allowed into schools. The underlying message, they say, is that schools are endorsing these products and brands and encouraging a captive audience of students to be good consumers. Advertising critic Jean Kilbourne says, "It's a very dangerous thing for a corporation to have this kind of presence in school." A commercial message in school has "an aura of responsibility and truth," she says, because children tend to believe that what they learn in school is valid.[12]

Shop 'Til You Drop

It used to be that kids were pretty much uninterested in shopping until they became teens. Mothers of a generation or so ago will tell you that they could purchase generic jeans and T-shirts for their preteens who would wear them without much protest. Now, the shopping lifestyle with its intense focus on trends and what's cool has gripped the tweenaged set, especially young girls. This obsession is promoted and glorified in the media they watch.

Children voted "Lizzie McGuire," a Disney production, as their favorite television show in the 2003 Kids' Choice Awards run by Nickelodeon each year. To capitalize on the show's popularity, Disney also produced a PG-rated spin-off, "The Lizzie McGuire Movie." Here's what film critic Roger Ebert had to say about the movie: "(It) celebrates popularity, beauty, great hair, lip gloss and overnight stardom, those universal obsessions of pop teenage culture. Lizzie herself obviously has never had a real idea in her silly little head … As a role model, Lizzie functions essentially as a spokeswoman for the teen retail fashion industry, and the most quoted line in the movie is likely to be when the catty Kate accuses (Lizzie) of being an 'outfit repeater.' Since many of the kids in the audience will not be millionaires and do indeed wear the same outfit more than once, this is a little cruel, but there you go."[13]

The actress who plays Lizzie is Hilary Duff, ranked as the most popular female star with kids 6 to 11 in a 2003 survey by Marketing Evaluations/TvQ. Duff's management announced plans to capitalize on her popularity by signing her up not only to make movies and a solo CD, but also to sell apparel, cosmetics, dolls, footwear, jewelry, and even pet products, such as collars and leashes, under the label, Stuff from Hilary Duff. Visa will offer a Hilary Duff prepaid card, that functions like a gift card, and plans to market it to 6- to 13-year-olds.[14]

Many more actors, athletes, and musicians who are popular with kids are no longer content with using their celebrity status to endorse just a few products as a sideline to their careers. Like Hilary Duff, they now aim to literally "brand" themselves to their target audience. In the tween market, no one has been as successful at this as Mary-Kate and Ashley Olsen, the twins who first debuted in the late 1980s as infants on the ABC sitcom "Full House." Their Dualstar Entertainment company markets videos, books, dolls, games, clothing, accessories, and cosmetics to the tune of $1 billion a year.

According to the Associated Press, "their books, which were first launched about ten years ago, have generated over $130 million in retail sales, and sold more than 30 million copies in print among four book series.

Mary-Kate and Ashley Olsen dolls, made by Mattel Inc., are the nation's no. 1 selling celebrity doll ..." Sales of their sportswear and accessories for tweens, hair care products, cosmetics, and toddler clothing at Wal-Mart generate $750 million annually. They have branched out into teen apparel and "envision adding women's, infant's, and boy's clothing, as well as expanding overseas to such markets as France, Germany, Mexico, and Japan."

Even so, Mary-Kate (who has a net worth of $150 million) told the AP, "We don't want to be too much in their faces. We don't want people to get sick of us."[15]

It's difficult to conjure up just what might be "too much" for these young marketing dynamos. But it's probably all too much for the parents of tween girls who are fans of the Olsen twins.

'Nothing to Wear'

One area where many parents feel they are fighting a losing battle is in the clothing that is marketed to tween girls. "This is the world of naked fashion," according to *The Washington Post*, "for girls from high school down

More than **three in five** 12- to 13-year-olds (62%) in a survey said that buying certain **products** made them **feel better** about themselves.

Source: Center for a New American Dream poll, May 2002

– even to elementary school – the less-is-more look flaunting breasts, bellies and bottoms. Many, if not most, schools forbid or discourage it, parents and teachers complain about fighting the 'whore wars,' and yet the trend shows no signs of letting go after a decade of growth."[16]

Newspapers across the country have reported on this "war" between parents and marketers. Here's some of what they've found in the girls' department at major retailers:

- Terry-cloth bikinis at GapKids
- Glitter on and in everything from denim skirts to lavender eye shadow
- Pedicure kits for 4- to 12-year-olds at Bath & Body Works
- Metallic-looking bras and bikini underpants at Sears
- Thong underwear for girls as young as seven at abercrombie, the kids' branch of youth-oriented Abercrombie and Fitch (The store ultimately removed these from shelves following an angry e-mail and letter campaign from parents.)

"We want to get them in, convert them, then keep them as long as possible," Kathy Bronstein, chief executive of Wet Seal Inc., which owns Zutopia, a tween retailer, told the *Los Angeles Times*.[17]

Most parents see this as the outrageous selling of sex to young children. Clothing designers and retailers defend the low-rise jeans and high-cut belly shirts as giving girls the clothing they demand. Joanne Arbuckle of the Fashion Institute of Technology in New York said, "This has been the trend for quite some time in girls sizes 7 to 14. It started with the Spice Girls and Britney Spears. The girls watch the entertainers and they want to mimic them. It is not for the industry to say you should be wearing this. We produce what our market would like to wear."[18]

According to market researchers, the trend started in the entertainment world with Madonna, followed by Spears, Jennifer Lopez, and Christina Aguilera. The teen fashion magazines popularized and equated the sexy dressing with "power." Retailers kept pushing the skimpy fashions to younger and younger girls.[19]

What parents see as too sexy, the girls just see as fashionable. "These clothes are cool, and everyone wears them," said one 11-year-old. "They're just clothes."[20]

Children ages 9-13 name these as their **number one** source of information about new styles of clothing:

Friends	59%
Television	58%
School	38%
Stores	31%

Source: *Inside Kids, Nickelodeon, April 1997*

Other girls deny that the clothing sends any message to boys. "If they're bothered, that's their problem," said one. Another agreed, saying "Girls have as much right to express themselves as boys do. It's not a girl's job either to please or keep the boys on track."[21]

Advertisers have sold this style of dressing to girls as rebellious and liberating. But psychologists and other child development experts scoff at the notion that the clothing denotes "power" or "liberation" and believe the trend creates moral and safety issues for girls. "The fashion industry is telling them what to do," said Lois Banner, a professor of gender studies at the University of Southern California. "I don't see the free choice in that at all. The clothes for little girls look like they were made for harlots or very sexualized women. They are tight, revealing, low-cut, and seem more appropriate for 25-year-old vamps looking for men. We are putting our girls at great risk." Preteen girls, she says, do not have the maturity to handle the attention that provocative clothing can draw.[22]

In the meantime, parents struggle to come up with strategies to thwart the body-revealing standard pushed by clothing retailers. Many complain that stores offer them little or no choice; they and their daughters can't find longer shorts or jeans that start at the waistline even when they try to. Some mothers have told us they now buy clothes a size or two larger than what their daughters regularly wear. Too many parents find themselves in the position of this mother: Shopping for a dress her daughter could wear to a school awards event, Mom refused to buy the spaghetti-strapped dress the girl wanted unless she agreed to wear a sweater over it. Arriving at school, they found that most of the girls were wearing dresses showing lots of skin. With a resigned sigh, Mom let her daughter remove the sweater.

Back-to-School Shopping Without Mom

According to the media and retailers, a small but growing trend is for tweens to be allowed to do at least some of their back-to-school shopping on their own or with friends rather than with either Mom or Dad along. Some parents, apparently, have opted out because of the time, stress, and tears involved. "There are so many other stresses between mothers and daughters," says one mother, "why add unnecessary ones?" Retailers have noticed. Limited Too, which caters to tweens, admits that its "stores are purposely overstuffed with merchandise and designed to look and feel a bit like every girl's disorganized bedroom." A marketing executive told *USA Today*, "Often, it will drive an adult crazy to be in our store."[23] In another trend, retailers are offering "experienced-based" stores that lure preteens as

Kids 8 to 18 spent an estimated $17 billion ($386 each) on bedroom décor in 2003.

Source: The WonderGroup consulting and marketing agency

"destinations." For example, the Club Libby Lu chain offers tweens pop star or princess "makeovers" complete with glitter lipstick and custom-mixed perfumes.

But is sending an 11-year-old off to the mall with several hundred dollars in her pocket the wisest parental decision? "We're sending our kids out to go shopping on their own, but everything they see or touch out there is designed to dazzle them," says Joline Godfrey, CEO of Independent Means, a company that sells products and services to parents who want to raise financially fit children. "It just seems immoral on some deep, primal level."[24] In the meantime, one of the independent tween shoppers that *USA Today* tracked blew her $200 in cash on "munchies" at the food court and just one outfit that included a $27 pink belt and $60 pink and black sneakers. The girl's Mom admitted that, "by October, she'll be saying she needs more."

The Legacy of Reese's Pieces

Back in the 1950s, large consumer companies like Procter & Gamble sponsored TV soap operas and then had their products featured in the story lines of the shows. This practice had more or less disappeared by the 1960s, however, and advertising and entertainment were kept separate for the next 20 years. That all changed in 1982 when a little boy laid down a trail of candy to lure an alien out of its hiding place in the phenomenally successful movie, "E.T. the Extra Terrestrial." Hershey's saw sales of its Reese's Pieces candy climb 65 percent following the movie's release.[25] (Mars, which makes M&Ms, had been offered the opportunity first and had refused.) Hollywood had rediscovered the gold mine of "product placement."

Entertainment for kids and adults is now littered with "embedded" advertising. Advertisers know that kids with remote controls can go channel surfing during commercial breaks so getting their products seen and plugged during the programming is an attractive alternative. On the TV talent show "American Idol," judges sipped from logo glasses of Coke while contestants awaited the verdict sitting on a Coca-Cola red sofa in the "Coca-Cola Room." After each song, the host reminded viewers they could vote on their AT&T Wireless cellular phones. Finalists arrived at the site of the competition in Ford SUV vehicles. No wonder "American Idol" was named one of the industry's "Top 10 Product Placement Award" winners in 2002.[26]

The Roxy Girl label sells beach and surfwear for preteen girls. It has now launched a series of books called "Luna Bay, The Roxy Girl Series" about a group of five 15-year-old girls who live and surf in the fictional seaside town of Luna Bay. Promoters of the books claim the goal is to get young girls to read more, but it's obviously also a ploy to sell more Roxy Girl fashions.[27]

Movies and particularly video games are also full of logos and brand-name merchandise. Both Intel and McDonald's paid to be included in the Sims Online game, part of the top-selling computer game franchise that features a virtual family that the player creates and manages. Some video game producers, however, use brand name products in their games and don't even ask marketers to pay for placement. They believe the branded products add to the realism of the game. Passengers in the "Crazy Taxi" video game ask the player to take them to Pizza Hut or KFC. Mike Fisher, vice president of entertainment marketing for Sega of America, explained, "It's a reflection of all the brands in our environment. You don't pick up a facial tissue, you pick up a Kleenex. You don't pick up a corn chip, you pick up a Frito or a Dorito. In the video game experience, you don't want to drive to the fried chicken restaurant, you want to drive to KFC."[28]

More than 20% of schools now offer brand-name fast food in their cafeterias.

Source: Centers for Disease Control

Online Advergames

Marketers have taken advantage of kids' love of electronic gaming with a new twist – it's called an "advergame." An advergame merges advertising with a computer game. For example, when Mattel introduced the "My Scene" Barbie doll with a bare midriff and cell phone to market to tween-aged girls, it created a TV commercial with a story line: Barbie's in a cab chatting on the phone. She gets out of the cab as a cute guy walks up to flag the cab down. The cab pulls away and Barbie frantically discovers that her phone is still inside. The TV ad ends with a "to be continued" line. But the story line can only be continued by going to the myscene.com Web site, as one million or so girls did in each of the months the ad aired. Twelve "Webisodes" featuring the doll followed.[29]

The Nickelodeon network's Web site, Nick.com, which gets two million unique visitors each week, is ranked number one for kids ages 2 to 14 by NetRatings. So when the network wanted to attract viewers for its new series, "Jimmy Neutron," it teamed up with Quaker Oats to create an online racing game. Kids needed to obtain a code from inside a cereal box that would give them access to the Web site, where they could build their own rocket. Half a million kids played the game, and the series' premiere was the network's highest-rated in history.[30]

"Advergames can reinforce a brand image, build a database of information about its users, directly target the market they want to hit – all very inexpensively when compared to what it costs to advertise in other media," according to *The Washington Post*. The advantage of an advergame is that instead of capturing only 30 to 60 seconds of advertising time in front of a potential consumer, the marketer may get an hour or more while the child plays the online game.

Eyes on Kids

Children ages 5 to 12 are the fastest growing segment of online users and arguably the most naïve when it comes to understanding the motives behind a lot of online content. Much of what passes for sweepstakes, promotions, chat rooms, and clubs on the Internet is actually research being done on kids by marketers. In exchange for giveaways, prizes, cash, or chances to win something, kids are asked to "register" or "fill out a survey," and in the process reveal information about themselves or their family. Children under the age of 13 are now protected by the Children's Online Privacy Protection Act (COPPA). This law took effect in 2000 and prohibits commercial Web sites from collecting personal information from children without parental consent and proper notification. (This law is under review by the U.S. Supreme Court.)

KidzEyes is a Web site run by Chicago-based C & R Research Services to survey children ages 6 to 14. The site is fully in compliance with COPPA, and kids cannot join unless their parents sign them up. The site states that only *aggregate* data about kids' survey responses is released to their clients, for example, "73% of Kidz between 8 and 10 years old like this

> **90% of kids over the age of 5 use computers. 59% use the Internet.**
> Source: U.S. Department of Education survey, September 2001

or that TV show." By completing surveys, kids can earn points that can be converted into cash or prizes. KidzEyes promises that they will "never, ever try to sell the Kidz anything."[31]

This site, however, *collects* a tremendous amount of personal data on the kids, their parents, and family. First, the parents must complete a survey of their own in order for the child to join the online panel. In addition to obtaining the name, street and e-mail addresses, phone number, and income level of the adult, the survey asks for the gender and ages of all children in the family; what kinds of computers, Internet connections, cable TV, video games, and DVD or VCR players the household has; what cereals, snack foods, fast-food meals and other products are purchased regularly; and what sports, hobbies, and other activities the kids enjoy. All this, before the child fills out his or her first survey!

Once the child has been signed up, he or she receives an e-mail invitation to participate in an online survey "at least once a month, and maybe more often." The company also conducts "chat-based surveys" where kids discuss topics in real time with an adult moderator. According to the Web site, "Kidz will be asked about things like TV shows for kids, movies, Web sites, snack foods, music, clothes, sports, video games and other things that kids are interested in. We'll have surveys about new products that haven't come out yet, and old, familiar products that Kidz may already know about. We'll ask about what Kidz like and don't like. We'll show Kidz ideas, and ask questions about what they think of them. And then we'll tell the manufacturers, programmers and Webmasters who send us their ideas how they look through our Kidz' eyes."[32] This is all stated in very respectful language, as if this were a service to kids. It's important to remember that this is simply an effort to help marketers sell children more stuff.

Even more enticing for kids are the rewards dangled in front of them for participating: "Usually a survey will take no more than 10 or 15 minutes to complete, and each of the Kidz taking it will receive 'KidzPoints.' One KidzPoint is worth 1 cent, and participation in most surveys will be worth anywhere from several hundred to a few thousand KidzPoints; the equivalent of $2 to $20, although some may be worth more and some less. Sometimes we'll run sweepstakes with really cool prizes. Sometimes we'll have cool games, screen savers, T-shirts and other things that we'll give away only to the Kidz on our panel. And from time to time we might run sweepstakes or offer other types of rewards to members of KidzEyes who refer their friends or neighbors to KidzEyes."[33]

It's not surprising that the Web site's research company reports that its surveys "routinely achieve response rates of 60%, and sometimes as high as 80%." The company offers potential clients "quick and easy access to kids and their parents" as well as to special groups of children: WhizKids, highly creative and articulate kids "great for idea development efforts," and Trendsetters, kids who are "on top of what's hot and what's not!"[34]

While it's easy to see why kids might clamor to join online panels like this one, we think parents need to seriously consider whether you want marketers to have such detailed information about your family and whether you want to contribute to the marketing onslaught against kids. Shouldn't we instead be trying to protect kids from it?

What Parents of Tweens Can Do

It's not unusual for parents of a smart-mouthed, surly tween to suddenly wonder whatever happened to their loving, obedient, and happy child. Tweens typically want to spend more time with their peers and seek more privacy and time alone when home. According to child psychologist Linda Sonna, they also realize for the first time that their parents are fallible, so tweens can often behave like disrespectful "little know-it-alls."[1] Despite their at-times obnoxious behavior, tweens do still value their parents. Author Linda Perlstein spent a year hanging out with suburban middle schoolers and she reports, "Twelve-year-olds don't want you to leave them alone. They want their relationship with you to shift a little, but they don't want you to go away."[2]

It's important that you as a parent model respectful behavior, give tweens appropriate time and space to grow toward independence, and remember that you are still the most important influence in their lives. Sonna recommends that parents make "a gradual transition from ... protecting and controlling during early childhood, to teaching and supervising during the tween ... years ..."3

Parents of tweens still need to be monitoring and limiting children's TV, video game, and Internet time, discussing what they're watching (including media such as movies, video games, and magazines) with them, and teaching them social skills. Now is not the time to abdicate your role to the media as the most important teacher your kids have! The social skills you should be modeling and teaching your tween will be more complex: They should include accepting decisions of authority, resisting peer pressure, disagreeing appropriately, setting appropriate boundaries, and following through on commitments.

Monitoring the media habits of tweens will be more difficult to do as they will have more access to a variety of media, not all appropriate for their age. That's why talking with your kids about what they're viewing and doing is so important. You want to be sure they are not "swallowing whole" the marketing and media messages they see. Help them develop critical thinking skills by asking questions, commenting on, and discussing with your kids what they view. Here are other things parents of tweens can do:

Set limits and boundaries.

Kids secretly crave boundaries; it reassures them that you love them and care about what happens to them. You're the parent. It's your role to set the rules that govern TV watching, what video games kids can play, how they may dress, and how much snack food they can consume. Even if your child has money from allowances, grandparents, gifts, or doing chores, you should still be the one to approve or disapprove what he or she can spend the money on. When you are setting up the rules you can discuss them with your child, but you make the ultimate decision. Also decide in what areas you are willing to let your child make choices. Make sure he or she knows what the rules are and that there will be consequences for breaking the rules. Your kids will be more likely to comply if they see you being fair and consistent.

Begin teaching your child how to save and spend money wisely.

If you give your child an allowance, make it dependent on him completing some daily or weekly household chores that are age-appropriate. Help your child open a savings account, and require that some percentage of the money she earns or receives goes into the account. With the money your child is allowed to spend, clearly explain what he or she may buy – which toys, clothes, or snacks. During the tween years, parents should still supervise kids' purchases. If your child asks you to buy, or wants to purchase with his own money, a costly item, help your child create a plan through which he can work and save toward some or all of the item's cost. No child should get everything he or she wants. Real life just doesn't work that way for most of us, and kids should learn the value in making smart choices early on. Be sure to model good spending and saving habits yourself.

Teach your child values.

Kids don't learn right from wrong in a vacuum. The Character Counts! organization tells parents they need to teach, enforce, advocate, and model good character traits to children. Teach – make sure your child knows what trustworthiness, respect, responsibility, fairness, caring, and good citizenship (the Six Pillars of Character) are and that you expect your child to demonstrate such behavior. Enforce – praise your child when you see such behavior and give consequences when kids fail to live up to these standards. Advocate – give your child reasons for why it is important to exhibit these character traits now and in the future; never be neutral about the importance of good character or casual about improper conduct. Model – make sure your behavior is consistent with what you expect of your child; set a good example. Kids who develop good values and character care about other people.[4]

Help your child resist peer pressure.

You want your child to have friends and fit in, but you also don't want him or her to be a slave to the crowd and every passing fad. We know a girl whose friends laughed at her for wearing the same sweater to school twice in one week. Other kids are targets of much crueler taunts and behavior from classmates because they're different in some way. Parents naturally ache for a child who suffers from the ridicule or exclusion of peers.

Encourage your child to pursue healthy friendships. Get to know your child's friends (and their parents, if possible). Welcome them into your home. Promote activities that require face-to-face social interaction, cooperation, and conversation. Research shows that if kids have trouble making friends, they have more mental health and social adjustment problems in later life. Having even one close friend, however, seems to shield children from these problems. Studies also show that popular children know how to "break the ice" with their peers, act positively with other children, and manage conflict constructively.[5] If you can help your child develop these social skills, it may help him or her weather superficial popularity standards based on clothing or other possessions.

Reassure your child that popularity is not an accurate predictor of future success or happiness in life. Point out and discuss examples when you can. Actress Reese Witherspoon, for example, has been quoted in many interviews as saying that she "was a total dork growing up." She told one magazine, "I knew I was smart. I didn't know I was pretty. And you know what? I don't think it's really that important. I see (my magazine covers), and I say, 'Who is this person?' I go in at the crack of dawn and somebody puts fake hair on your head, a bunch of makeup on your face, and dresses you in a multi-thousand dollar outfit. It's not like the pictures of me over my couch."[6]

Challenge your child to be creative in meeting the need to be cool instead of simply shopping for what he or she wants.

Trend watchers looking for cool kids often find them to be "do-it-yourselfers." Discuss this with your child. These kids redecorate their bedrooms using only paint, discarded furniture, or rummage sale finds. They perk up old T-shirts and jeans with buttons, ribbons, or lace trim, or they remake clothing found at garage sales and thrift stores. Coming up with low-cost projects like these, teaching your child a do-it-yourself skill, or hunting for bargains can be great ways to share time together.

Get involved with your child's school.

If you disagree with policies at your child's school that allow excessive marketing to students, let the school principal, the PTA, and the school board know. Ask them to solicit parents' opinions before they sign agreements for vending machines, cafeteria food service, computer hardware or software, Internet service, or other marketing-related ventures. Increased attention to the rising rate of childhood obesity has led schools and some food companies to reverse earlier marketing decisions. New York City's Education Department and the Los Angeles school system have banned soda and candy from school vending machines. Kraft Foods announced that it would no longer advertise processed food on Channel One. Use these as examples when talking to school officials.

Find out if the local school has a dress code, and if it does, discuss it with your child and how you can help him or her comply with it. Some public and private schools have found that school uniforms help mask socioeconomic differences among students and reduce peer pressure when it comes to brand-name clothing. The U.S. Department of Education offers information on school uniform policies at www.ed.gov/updates/uniforms.html. Despite some opposition to dress codes and uniform requirements, the courts have generally upheld schools' rights to enforce them.

Amazing as it may seem, you may also need to check out the appropriateness of school staff clothing. Some school administrators have had to create staff dress policies because young, newly hired teachers sometimes show up for work with visible tattoos and bellybutton rings or in low-rise jeans and halter tops. If this is happening in your child's school, you and other parents may need to work with the principal to demand that all teachers be good role models and command kids' respect by dressing professionally.

Monitor your child's activity on the computer and the Internet.

Teach your child how to evaluate Web sites on the Internet and their purpose: Are they selling a product or promoting a point of view? Encourage your child to ask you if he has questions about anything he encounters online. Place the computer your child uses where you can easily check on how he or she is using it. Be aware that current law requires marketers to get parental permission before signing up kids under 13 for online clubs, panels, or advisory boards. And then consider these carefully before allowing your child to join them. Talk with your child about the purpose of these "clubs" and why your family might not want to reveal personal information to marketers.

Set up an agreement or contract with your child that sets out the conditions under which he or she uses the computer. It might include when and how long the child can be on the Internet and what kind of or which sites he is allowed to enter. Your child should also agree not to give out her name, parent's name, address, phone number, or credit card information without parental permission. Consider using blocking software that can prevent your child from sending out family data. Information for parents on many Internet privacy and safety techniques and software tools is available on the helpful Web site www.getnetwise.org.

Consider setting up a "dress code" for your daughter.

If your daughter pressures you to buy or has bought for herself clothing you consider to be inappropriate for her, set some rules. First, you need to have a conversation about why you feel certain clothing is wrong for her. Help her understand that clothing sends a message about the wearer, whether or not it's what the wearer intended. Explain why skimpy clothing is *not* a "power" statement for a young girl and could even place her in danger. With her input, if possible, decide what she can and cannot wear. Most importantly, teach your child to judge others by what's on the inside and not what's on the outside – to value character rather than appearance and clothing.

Do some research and find stores that offer trendy clothing without the bare or sexy look. Some retailers seem to be getting the message about parents' frustration. *Time* magazine profiled Pacific Sunwear, a successful teen clothing chain that sells the hottest surfer/skater looks: "Though the chain's merchandise looks cutting edge, (CEO Greg) Weaver is quite careful to avoid fashion extremes. Unlike Abercrombie and Fitch, which plays up the libidinous elements of its teen offerings, PacSun sells clothes that would pass muster at any high school with a dress code. Weaver says he avoids resorting to sexual advertising messages to move merchandise. 'Many teenagers love it,' he says, 'but why would I alienate the parents? I can't forget my customer is 15 and doesn't have a credit card.'"[7]

Enlist the help of other parents and the school, if you can. Friends are so important to kids as well as being their primary source of information on clothing that, if you can get a group of parents working together with their girls, getting your child to dress appropriately will be much easier. We've spoken at events organized by mothers for their daughters that included a fashion show. Retailers like Gap and Target contributed clothing that helped demonstrate to the girls how to be fashionable yet modest. We saw girls responding very positively to this approach.

Have regular "family nights."

One night a week, turn off the TV, the CD player, and the computer. Play "low-tech" board or card games. Cook dinner together and have a picnic on a blanket in the living room or on the front porch. Plan a weekend outing or your summer vacation. Put a jigsaw puzzle together. Drink lemonade in the back yard, gaze at the stars, and just talk. The point is to create a quiet space where family members can enjoy each other and build relationships.

Get your child involved in a community service activity.

The options here are many for your child. He or she could:

- Help serve a meal at a homeless shelter.
- Organize the family's recycling efforts.
- Visit a nursing home.
- Join a group to pick up trash along the highway.
- Tutor a younger child.

Discuss with your child what he or she learned from the experience. Give praise and point out how the child's efforts served other people or a greater good. Ask the child to come up with ideas for other ways to help people.

Head for the great outdoors.

According to Michael M. Brown, an outdoor media and marketing specialist in Ohio, 96 percent of

American kids have never fished, hunted, or even hiked in the woods. "Kids ... don't know that eggs come from chickens," he says.[8] What you can do is locate hiking and biking trails, state and local parks, zoos, wildlife refuges, and other outdoor attractions in your area. Then arrange for family outings to take advantage of these opportunities with family picnics, swims, hikes, bike rides, or camping trips. Nurturing a love of nature and enjoyment of the outdoors in your children may help ease their addiction to material possessions.

Why Marketers
Love Teens

7

Natalie, a 17-year-old, works 30 hours a week and spends all of her pay on clothes and cosmetics.

• • •

Shawn, 15 years old, has been picked up for shoplifting twice. He says he "deserves" to have what other kids have, but he doesn't have the money to buy, so he steals.

• • •

Sixteen-year-old Heather told her parents she wants breast implants for her birthday. She's been thinking about it for years.

• • •

These are kids we know who, in one way or another, have been seduced by the messages of advertisers. Marketers often refer to how "savvy" teens are when it comes to advertising. The flood of ads they are exposed to, says Michael Wood, vice president of Teen Research Unlimited (TRU), "means a sophistication on the part of teens. They're savvier consumers, and they're much more conscious of how advertisers are courting them. They can see right through it."[1]

But child experts say that despite being more knowledgeable about advertising, teens are still very susceptible to it. "Research suggests that understanding advertising techniques does not diminish its strong influence on (teens') choice of products. This is not surprising since advertising often appeals more to emotion than intellect," a coalition of more than 50 scholars and leaders in pediatric health care, education, and child advocacy wrote in a letter that was sent to presidential candidates in 2000.[2]

The American Academy of Child & Adolescent Psychiatry lists these feelings and behaviors as *normal* for teens in the middle school and early high school years:[3]

- Struggle with sense of identity
- Feeling awkward or strange about one's self and one's body
- Focus on self, alternating between high expectations and poor self-concept
- Interests and clothing style influenced by peer group

- Moodiness
- Complaints that parents interfere with independence
- Tendency to return to childish behavior, particularly when stressed
- Mostly interested in the present; limited thoughts of future
- Concerns regarding physical and sexual attractiveness to others
- Rule and limit testing
- Frequently changing relationships
- Worries about being normal

Couple these susceptibilities with the enormous spending power of 32 million American teens and it's

Three in **four** teens polled said they planned to **work** during the school year. Here is what they said they would spend their money on:

Entertainment	57%
Clothing	50%
Automobile	41%
College savings	33%
Investments	16%

Source: Junior Achievement/Harris Interactive Poll, 2003

easy to see why teens are so attractive to marketers: In a lackluster U.S. economy in 2002, teens spent more than $170 billion, up from $150 billion in 2000.[4] According to a Teen Research Unlimited study, teen consumers in 2002 spent an average of $101 per week, combining their own discretionary spending with any spending they did on their parents' behalf for personal or household items.

While teens are a lucrative market, they are also a challenging one for advertisers for several reasons. This generation of teens is known for

- "multi-tasking."
- short attention spans.
- marketing cynicism.

Multi-Tasking Teens

Teens are known to be "early adopters" of new technologies. Growing up with computers, game consoles, CD and DVD players, and portable devices, teens move easily among media options. Researchers and marketers now observe that teens very often "multi-task" – that is, they engage in several media or communications activities at the same time. MTV's research finds "young people are no longer bound by the confines of the calendar day, because their constant multi-tasking and communication now permits them to squeeze 31 hours into a 24-hour day. ... (W)e're talking about a generation of people that can surf the Web, watch television, actively participate in an online chat room and talk on the phone simultaneously."[5]

Advertisers may be sending marketing messages aimed at teens through all of these media outlets, but if a teen is engaged in three or four activities at the same time, is he or she paying attention to any of the ads? Marketers have to find unconventional ways to break out of the clutter of ads that surround teens everywhere.

Always Moving On

Teens are used to a world of endless choices, in TV channels, games, Web sites, etc. As a result, says Betty Frank, executive vice president of research for MTV Networks, "they're used to getting what they want when they want it. So they're impatient. They move around a lot. They have short attention spans."[6]

Reality TV is a big hit with teens. Programmers believe it's because the short duration of the shows, four to 13 weeks, and the story arcs (a quick beginning, middle and end) appeal to them. Teens, so concerned with being cool, move from fad to fad, sometimes so fast that the mass marketers can't keep up. "The very nature of cool is that not everybody's in on it, so once people know about it, it's hard to stay cool," says trend watcher Jon Hein. "The shelf life shrinks."[7]

There is now an industry of trend watchers, people who follow, question, observe, and videotape young people they've judged to be cool. They get teens to fill out lengthy surveys in shopping malls, follow them home, interview them on camera, dig through their closets, and shoot photos of them at bars, raves, and concerts. Then they disseminate the collected information to marketers who are willing to pay a lot of money for the latest tips on what's in and what's out. For example, corporations fork over $15,000 for an annual subscription to the *Hot Sheet,* a publication of the Zandl Group.[8] Even with the help of trend watchers, it's become a frantic race for marketers to get new products out there fast enough to catch fads before they become passé. In order to keep up with what's cool, teens must spend an excessive amount of time and money.

Cynical and Savvy

Because this generation of kids has been the target of marketers since infancy, they can be very cynical about advertising. Says TRU's Wood, "Because they've been bombarded with ads every day of their life, they're savvy. They're spending a lot of money, but they see through the hype. They can't stand being ripped off."[9] Teens also don't like to see themselves as being manipulated or told what to do, especially by adults. And they reject advertising that seems to do so.

To overcome these barriers in reaching teens, marketers have devised ways of selling to teens that go far beyond the traditional mass market advertising seen on TV or radio, in magazines, or on billboards. Marketers call these new approaches:

- viral marketing,
- guerrilla marketing,
- and underground marketing.

Viral Marketing

While teens don't like to feel that they're being manipulated by adults, they *are* heavily influenced by their peers. Market research has revealed that certain teens are trendsetters; they are the first to adopt something new and other teens tend to follow their lead when it comes to opinions about a new product. Researchers have different names for these teens – influencers, connectors, trendsetters – but marketers covet them because if they like a product, they can create the word-of-mouth "buzz" that spurs sales. This type of marketing succeeds because it gives the illusion that kids themselves have decided the product is cool, not the big corporate marketer. Actually, in one way or another, the marketer is paying the "trend-setting" teen to spread the word.

In an average week, **76%** of teens go to the **shopping mall,** usually spending more than four hours there.

Source: Teen Research Unlimited

Proctor & Gamble carefully selects up to 200,000 teens for a group it calls Tremor. Tremor members are solicited for their opinions on products like Cover Girl cosmetics about twice a month in exchange for chances to win prizes and get a sneak peek at new products. They are then asked to spread the word to their friends.[10] On the Web, some companies have offered free e-mail or home pages to teens. The payback comes whenever a teen sends an e-mail; an ad and a link to the company's Web site goes with it.

Another ploy used by advertisers is to create edgier or racier ads than those allowed on television and put them on Web sites. Then the sites allow the viewer to e-mail the ads to friends. These ads have promoted everything from noodles and beer to Xbox and condoms. The beer ads, sponsored by Anheuser-Busch, feature "jokey, child-like sketches ... more like the kind of cartoons normally aimed at kids and teenagers. Only Web visitors listing a birth date indicating they are over 21 are admitted to the site," according to *Advertising Age*.[11] A marketing expert noted, however, that kids as young as 10 are able to maneuver through the age check.

Guerrilla Marketing

Guerrilla marketing is advertising a product in an unusual or unpredictable way or placing a "product in the target's hands in unexpected places."[12] Nike displayed a new line of shoes in a trendy New York City art gallery before blitzing teens with ads on teen-oriented TV channels and Web sites. Nintendo sent teams of "human interactives" out on the streets in major cities with flat-screen monitors attached to the front of their bodies. Consumers were able to test the new GameCube on the spot. Other companies have sent mascots dressed as snack foods out to distribute samples to passersby. L.A. Gear sponsored an MTV Museum of Rock & Roll show that traveled to shopping malls all over the country.

To advertise its Raging Cow flavored milk drinks, Dr Pepper created a Weblog, a self-published Web diary written from the point of view of the cow mascot. Then it offered teenaged "bloggers" gift certificates and other prizes for trying the drinks and writing about them in their own Weblogs. Dunkin' Donuts hired students attending the NCAA basketball tournament to shave the company logo onto their heads. At the Boston Marathon, Reebok paid 100 students to wear temporary tattoos and to convince another 1,000 at the race to wear the marketing tattoo for free. TV networks have tried all sorts of stunts to market new programs, from pasting shark decals in hotel pools (for Discovery's "Shark Week") and towing banners behind helicopters flying over public beaches to inserting promotional messages into fortune cookies and on the lids of pizza boxes.

Underground Marketing

In this type of marketing (also called "stealth marketing"), advertising is presented in such a way that people don't even realize that what they've seen is an ad. "Get your target talking about your brand without even knowing they're talking about it ... now that's real buzz," says the Web site for Big Fat, a New York-based firm that specializes in underground marketing.[13] Knowing that kids watch their peers closely for new clothing trends, fashion retailers have begun paying influential teens to wear their clothing. Other companies have paid teens to talk about their products in chat rooms and in their instant messaging with friends. Managers at the Gap and Abercrombie and Fitch watch for attractive teens with a certain "look" to enter their stores and then offer them jobs as sales clerks. Sony Ericsson hired actors to pose as tourists asking people to take their picture using a new mobile photo phone. Of course, once the photo was taken, the actors struck up a conversation focused on how cool the phone was.

Sometimes teens are recruited unknowingly into underground marketing schemes. *The New York Times Upfront* magazine reported, "(O)ne New York marketing firm set up fake Web sites with deliberately lax security that allowed hackers to think they had broken into unedited scenes from upcoming movies. The result: The hackers sent the footage to dozens or even hundreds of friends, becoming an advertising vehicle for the movies without knowing it."[14] Because of the stealthy tactics used, underground marketing may be the most deceptive advertising of all.

Musical Hucksters

Celebrities have been paid to pitch products for years. About a hundred years ago, Buffalo Bill Cody enthusiastically endorsed Kickapoo Indian Oil for Rheumatism. More recently, Michael Jackson and Madonna both rather infamously flogged Pepsi. (Jackson's hair caught fire while filming a Pepsi commercial, and Pepsi pulled its Madonna ad after she released a highly controversial music video.) Michael

Jordan has promoted everything from hot dogs to underwear. Dozens of celebrities have sported milk mustaches. And of course, athletic shoe companies pay millions to sign up sports superstars.

Today, more than ever, celebrities are not only hawking products for other corporations, but are creating their own product lines that feed off of their name and image or using a variety of marketing channels to advertise and brand themselves. Let's look at musicians as an example. Music is a powerful influence in the lives of teens. Research shows that teens listen to music because they identify with the messages in lyrics. They associate emotional highs and lows with the music that seems to speak to or reflect those moments.[15] These strong associations give popular musicians a lot of clout with teens.

> Bob Pittman, founder of MTV, to Ralph Nader, consumer activist: "Ralph, we don't influence 14-year-olds, we OWN them."
>
> Source: "Interview with Joseph Chilton Pearce" in Journal of Family Life magazine, Vol. 5, No. 1, 1999

As radio play for new artists has become more restricted and promotion by record labels less reliable, musicians have turned to cross-marketing and advertising to promote their music. "Pop musicians are taking their top 40 hits to TV ads," notes *USA Today*. "Musical artists used to view commercial use of their songs as taboo, forcing marketers to wait years to use those songs in ads. But an oversupply of artists and a 13 percent decline in worldwide album sales since 2001 are forcing musicians to sing a new tune."[16] Also contributing to the decline of sales are Internet file-sharing, illegal down-loading, and CD burning.

Artists are now willing to time the release of a new CD to meet the needs of an advertiser:

- The singer Jewel and her label, Atlantic Records, agreed to release a new album with her song, "Intuition," to coincide with the launch of Schick's new Intuition razor for women with ads using the song as their theme.

- Pepsi's ad featuring Beyonce Knowles was aired at the same time her first album came on the market.

- Smashmouth agreed to perform at an event for Jeep; Jeep offered the group a Wrangler for use in a video of its new single. Jeep then decided to put the song in a TV ad campaign running just as the album was released.

- Even Madonna, no longer assured of instant record chart success, agreed to vamp on camera in Gap corduroys while singing "Hollywood" from her new album.

"Advertising is the new radio," claims James Mahoney, music director for ad agency Foote Cone & Belding.[17]

Corporate sponsorship of concert tours has been commonplace since 1981 when Jovan, a musk oil com-pany that was struggling at the time, paid $500,000 to sponsor a Rolling Stones tour. The resulting publicity for

Jovan, "put them on the map in a major way," says Jay Coleman, founder of Entertainment Marketing Communications Inc.[18] For a recent tour, the Stones picked up Budweiser, Sprint, Tommy Hilfiger, and T-Mobile as sponsors. Christine Aguilera has corporate deals with Sketchers, Target, and Mattel; a Paul McCartney tour was promoted by Visa International; Jay-Z signed with Heineken USA and Reebok. The list goes on and on.

No group of musicians is as enmeshed with advertising as the rappers. Hip-hop music is saturated with product references. It started with rappers referring to favorite products in their songs with no payment involved. Run-DMC started the trend with their song, "My Adidas." The delighted shoe company saw thousands of fans waving their shoes in the air at a Run-DMC concert in 1986 and rewarded the group with a sponsorship deal worth about $1.5 million. Then Busta Rhymes had a hit record with "Pass the Courvoisier," and the resulting substantial increase in U.S. sales of the pricey cognac caught the attention of marketers again. Nelly landed a shoe contract after he recorded a paean to Nike's Air Force Ones. "Hip hop is aspirational and more open to identifying itself with brands," says Jameel Haasan Spencer, president of Blue Flame, a marketing

> **Girls ages 12 to 18 spend more than $37 billion each year on clothes.**
>
> Source: Teen Research Unlimited

and advertising company owned by rapper Sean "P. Diddy" Combs.[19]

Many rappers, including Eminem, Ice-T, Snoop Dogg, Master P, and Nelly have also created their own clothing lines. Jay-Z, co-owner of Roc-a-fella Records, purchased the U.S. rights to Armadale Vodka and encourages the record label's artists to mention it in their songs. Roc-a-fella CEO Damon Dash has been quoted as saying, "We know what kind of influence we have over our demographic, and we like to capitalize on every opportunity."[20]

The product pitching has become so incessant that MTV, "a company rarely shy about corporate sponsorships, says it's tired of airing commercials masquerading as music videos. The cable music channel has reportedly issued new guidelines that could make it difficult for artists to release videos in which products take center stage – particularly those to which the artist has financial ties," according to *Plugged In* magazine. The guidelines, however, likely won't stop the fusion of music and marketing that both sides find so lucrative. "If we're smart enough with our production design," says Mark Humphrey, a product broker with Band Ad Media, "we can slide by them left and right. It's like drugs across the border."[21]

The relentless beat of commercialism in today's music has parents and professionals worried, particularly when products like alcohol are presented in enticing ways to teen audiences. It's "corporate synergy spelled

S-I-N," says Joseph Califano, chairman of the National Center on Addiction and Substance Abuse at Columbia University. "These guys have a level of influence on teenagers that is second only to parents and schools. I think it's outrageous."[22]

Alcohol Advertising

Alcohol industry marketers vehemently deny that they target teens with advertising. "We'll gag at a gnat and swallow a camel before we advertise in anything that's major thrust is under-drinking-age people," Roger Brashears, Jr., promotions director for Jack Daniels, colorfully claims.[23] But study after study has found that kids and teens both see a lot of alcohol advertising and admit to being influenced by it. Here is some of what research has found:

- Teenagers have seen about 75,000 ads for alcohol by the time they turn 16.[24]

- 56 percent of students in grades 5 to 12 say that alcohol advertising encourages them to drink.[25]

- After just one year of advertising, children were almost as familiar with the frogs' "Bud-weis-er"

Kids see more commercials for **beer** than for sneakers, gum, or jeans. There were **208,909** alcohol commercials on TV in 2001.

Source: Center on Alcohol Marketing and Youth, Georgetown University

slogan as they were with Bugs Bunny's greeting, "What's up, Doc?"[26]

- Children who are more aware of TV beer ads have more favorable attitudes toward drinking, greater knowledge of beer brands, and an increased intention to drink as adults.[27]

- Young people begin to consume alcohol around the age of 13, and a large majority will do their heaviest drinking before their 21st birthday.[28]

According to a 2003 report by Georgetown University's Center on Alcohol Marketing and Youth, consumer surveys show that teenagers see more alcohol advertising than adults do. And black youth see more than 75 percent more alcohol ads in magazines than other youth do. The report also said that black youth are more likely to hear radio ads for alcohol than their peers, and that alcohol companies spent almost $12 million in 2002 advertising on the 15 television shows most popular with black youth, including "The Bernie Mac Show," "The Simpsons," "King of the Hill," and "George Lopez."

A lot of the ads depict drinking in a young, hip social scene. Sports broadcasting is heavily associated with beer ads. And we've already talked about how hip-hop artists are promoting not only beer but also hard liquor brands. The industry may deny that its marketing targets teenagers, but all of these associations make alcohol consumption enticing to teens. Adding money to the mix has been found to lead young people to substance abuse. A

Almost **20** million students said they would attend proms in 2003, with the average couple spending more than **$1,200**. Teens spend **$416** million a year for limousines, and **$172** million on flowers.

Source: Conde Nast, publisher of "Your Prom" magazine

2003 survey of 12- to 17-year-olds by the National Center on Addiction and Substance Abuse found that those who had $25 or more a week to spend were nearly twice as likely to drink, use drugs, and smoke, and more than twice as likely to get drunk as those with less spending money.

In September 2003, the Beer Institute and Distilled Spirits Council voluntarily agreed to place their ads only in media where 70 percent or more of the audience is 21 or older. The previous industry standard had been 50 percent. The change came following reports on alcohol marketing and underage viewers by the Federal Trade Commission and the National Academy of Science's Institute of Medicine and National Research. According to *Advertising Age,* the change would affect several magazines (such as *ESPN the Magazine, Rolling Stone, Vibe,* and *Spin*) and some hip-hop and urban radio stations; most television programming already adheres to the higher standard. A few sports shows, including "WWE Smackdown," fall below the 70 percent threshold.[29]

While the change is commendable, its net effect may be only minimal because most alcohol advertising had already been concentrated in media that meet the new standard. (Even an audience that is 70 percent over the age of 21 can include millions of children and teens who are still being exposed to alcohol advertising.)

An alcohol product that has come under fire from foes of underage drinking are Zippers, packaged cups of fruit-flavored gelatin that contain 12 percent alcohol per serving. Critics say the product, which is available in 22 states, looks too much like lunchbox snacks popular with children. Nick Costanzo, vice president of BPNC Inc., the Ohio company that manufactures Zippers, says the gelatin shots have never been aimed at minors and that instead the product "regulates and makes it safer to consume" a concoction that's been popular for years. Diane Riibe, executive director of Project Extra Mile, a Nebraska group working to get the gelatin shots banned, counters, "Everything about the product itself says nothing but 'kid.'"[30]

Parents and drug and alcohol counselors have also been critical of some candy products, such as tequila-flavored lollipops that include a real worm. The candy has no alcohol and is clearly marketed to kids. "Kids like gross things," says Paige Farmer, director of an alcohol prevention program in Maine. "The insect is a marketing tool targeted toward kids. They like it because it grosses out their parents. The fact there is an alcohol association is a big negative." Andrea Warren, a substance abuse counselor for adolescents, thinks the candy sends a message to kids that drinking is OK. "That lollipop is completely counterproductive to what everyone is doing to battle underage drinking," she says.[31]

Teens on the Web

By 2001, nearly three-quarters of all teens were online.[32] Advocates of computers and Internet access for kids at home and in school have stressed the educational benefits. Undeniably, the World Wide Web allows kids to do things barely thought possible even 10 years ago – collect research from primary sources all over the world, peer over the shoulders of scientists as they conduct experiments anywhere from Antarctica to

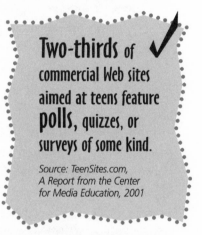

Two-thirds of commercial Web sites aimed at teens feature **polls**, quizzes, or surveys of some kind.

Source: TeenSites.com, A Report from the Center for Media Education, 2001

outer space, or organize national fund drives for children suffering in war-torn countries. But far more of the Web content designed for teens is about entertainment than information, commercialism than altruism. That's what a 2001 study of teen-oriented Web sites by the Center for Media Education found.

The Center's report states, "The lion's share of teen Web site content revolves around the popular culture that young people so avidly consume as well as the personal issues that tend to be foremost in their minds. Topping the list in our survey were music (found on 67.9 percent of the sites), film (54.3 percent), relationships (51.9 percent), advice (49.4 percent), and fashion (43.2 percent). At the other end of the spectrum were these topics that appeared on only a small percentage of commercial sites: religion (16 percent), travel (11.1 percent), food (11.1 percent), voluntarism (11.1 percent), the environment (6.2 percent), and nature (2.5 percent). ...

"Communication features – including message boards, chat rooms, and e-mail – are among the most dominant features of teen Web sites. Nearly three-quarters of the commercial sites in our survey offered bulletin or message boards; almost 60 percent provided chat opportunities, and nearly half offered free e-mail services. Some provide even more elaborate options for online communications, including virtual 'pen pals' and instant messaging – enabling teens to carry on a conversation with one or more friends without interrupting their other Web surfing activities – and customized 'e-cards' that can be sent directly to a friend's e-mail address on demand. Other online applications help teens manage their active social lives, with many sites allowing users to set up personalized calendars, address books, and voice mail. Social interaction, in fact, has become the primary reason most teens use the Web."[33]

Ninety percent of the commercial sites surveyed "encourage teenagers to become involved in the creation of content on the site."[34] Many sites help kids create their own home pages and show them how to copy images, content, and audio and video feeds from other sites or scan their own photos in order to paste them onto their personal pages.

In many respects, home pages, chat rooms, and instant messaging serve the same functions as teens' diaries, bedroom walls, bulletin boards, and phone calls. Kids often say things in chat rooms or post essays, poetry, or artwork on home pages that reveal intensely personal thoughts, feelings, and experiences. What they may not realize is the intense corporate scrutiny that these public discussions and postings get. "The Web has become a potent surveillance tool that enables constant and unobtrusive monitoring of teen subcultures."[35]

As we've seen, marketers have figured out how to take advantage of teens' adoption of the Internet as a primary communication tool – getting products mentioned in teen chat rooms can be far more effective than paying for a banner ad on a teen Web site. And market research may prove to be more lucrative than advertising for online companies looking for reliable sources of revenue.[36]

(No) Privacy Online

Unlike children under 13, teenagers aren't protected by law when it comes to Web sites collecting personal information. A Web site can collect data from any teen 13 or older without parental notification or consent. A teen can register on these sites by submitting his or her e-mail address, gender, birth date, and zip code. Bolt.com and gURL.com are two sites that seem quite typical of those sites aimed at teens. Both offer "privacy" policies telling teens they won't disclose or sell any "personally identifiable" information to other companies. But they warn teens that anything visitors post on their bulletin boards or in chat rooms, including personal information, can be viewed by any other visitor.

The goal of sites like these is clearly to gather as much data on teens as possible. The sites are crowded with polls, quizzes, games, questions asking visitors for feedback, sweepstakes, product reviews, bulletin boards, chat rooms, and other features that engage kids with their interactivity. Bolt.com is blatantly commercial – clicking on a new page always triggers a new pop-up or floating ad. On a single day, its home page included three Sony ads plus ads for Yahoo, Cingular phones, a college abroad program, and a movie DVD, a link to clothing retailer Marshalls (that lets you try fashions on a model), and an offer to get "special e-mail" from (pick your favorite) 7 UP, Sunkist, Hawaiian Punch, or A&W.

The gURL.com site plays to teen girls' obsession with their looks (body image, fashion, and style), relationships (dating, friends and family, sex), insecurities ("sucky emotions" defined as anger, depression, fear, feeling bored, heartbreak, and jealousy), and pop culture (music, movies, media, sports). Both sites lure teens by being deliberately provocative and heavily into content that deals with sexuality and sexual relationships. Neither site appears to screen or edit content posted by visitors. Bolt.com features selected postings from its bulletin boards on its "topic" pages. A recent example on the site's "dealing & advice" section page: "I f--- girls that smoke cigarettes." Girls and guys were asked what they "like about their butts" on a gURL.com message board. Much of the content on both sites, we believe, is highly inappropriate for younger teens.

Teens and Credit

According to *The New York Times,* 31.6 million teens spent $155 billion of their own money in 2000. To feed this appetite for purchasing, more and more teens hold part-time jobs. Sometimes these jobs can seriously cut into a teen's time with family and friends, homework, and school activities. We don't think it's healthy for working teens to be motivated only by the desire for more spending cash without having other goals such as saving for higher education.

Credit card and other companies are creating ways to make it easier for teens to shop without cash. Web companies like Cybermoola and RocketCash offer

One in five young people under the age of 20 have their own **credit cards** or access to their parents' credit cards. **14%** have their own debit cards.

Source: "How to Balance Teens, Credit Cards," msnbc.com, June 3, 2003 prepaid accounts for teens that operate like debit cards when shopping online. Kids can save and spend through a Doughnet account as well as earn money by answering polls. Visa Buxx and Citibank's Citicash prepaid cards are specifically marketed to teens and their parents.

While the prepaid cards prevent teens from getting into debt by buying on credit, marketers see them as a way to introduce kids to buying via a plastic card. "What the credit card industry tries to do is to simply get those students into their databanks so they know exactly when they're 18 years old, and they will immediately send them an application for a normal credit card," says Robert Manning, a Rochester Institute of Technology professor who studies consumer behavior.[37] Children as young as 13 as well as college students can find themselves inundated with credit card offers. Spending without thinking about how to pay off their bills, some young people accumulate thousands of dollars of debt on the cards by the time they graduate. (Thirteen percent of American college students owe between $3,000 and $7,000 in credit card debt.)[38]

Surveys have shown that 40 percent of teens are likely to buy something they really want, such as a pair of jeans, even if they don't have the money to pay for it. These free-spending habits, developed by teens and carried over into young adulthood, have serious consequences. The fastest growing age group for declaring bankruptcy is people under 25 years old.[39]

8

What Parents of Teens Can Do

"*I cried because I had no shoes, until I met a man who had no feet.*"
– Persian proverb

● ● ●

In today's affluent, consumer society, one of the most important yet difficult messages you need to convey to children is that having money and buying things will not necessarily make them happy. In fact, being excessively materialistic will probably make them *unhappy!* To teach your child that lesson, of course, you must first believe it yourself. Do you?

A majority of American teens don't. Three in four (almost twice as many as in 1970) believe it is "very important" to "essential" that they become "very well off financially."[1] And although most people (89 percent in a survey by Princeton sociologist Robert Wuthnow) believe American society is too materialistic, 84 percent still wish they had more money and 78 percent said it is "very or fairly important" to have "a beautiful home, a new car and other nice things."

Despite the fact that, statistically, Americans are more than twice as affluent today as they were in 1957, those who say they are "very happy" has actually declined over that time from 35 to 32 percent. Social psychologist and author, David G. Myers, of Hope College, calls this "soaring wealth and shrinking spirit 'the American paradox.' More than ever we have big houses and broken homes, high incomes and low morale, secured rights and diminished civility. We excel at making a living but often fail at making a life. We celebrate our prosperity but yearn for purpose. We cherish our freedoms but long for connection. In an age of plenty, we feel spiritual hunger."[2]

According to Myers, our thirst for consumption is attributable to two things: the way we constantly adapt to higher levels of affluence and our need to compare ourselves to others, usually to those who have more than we do. It's why kids now demand entertainment centers (color TV, computer, Internet connection, and PlayStation) in their own bedrooms while their grandparents were thrilled to have a black-and-white television set in the communal living room.

But if possessions don't have the power to make us happy, what does? University of Illinois psychologist Ed Diener and his son, Robert Biswas-Diener, have studied the "subjective well-being," or reported happiness, of people across many cultures and nations. Among the homeless in California, they found that what these people missed most were "not physical things such as good housing, but close and trusting friendships." A similar study in Calcutta, India, found that while the homeless there were actually physically worse off than the California homeless, "they were not as dissatisfied with life because they are more likely to have a strong social network." In fact, Diener says one of the most important findings of his research is that "the happiest people all seem to have good friends."[3]

That is what we need to believe ourselves and to impart, by our actions and our words, to our teenagers – that making, keeping, and cherishing relationships with others is the key to being happy. What can you do as a parent to moderate the allure of materialism in your teen's life and emphasize the importance of friends and family? Some suggestions follow.

Help your child achieve the right balance among school, work, and play.

Is your teen performing at least adequately in school? If not, you may have to help set up a schedule that sets adequate time aside for homework and reading. Does she participate in any extracurricular activities such as sports, music, or student government? Encourage children to join activities that will broaden their interests and introduce them to new friends and helpful, trustworthy adults. How many hours does he spend on the computer or playing video games? If you think the time is excessive, negotiate an agreement with your teen that sets guidelines on when and how long electronic games can be played. Or the agreement can outline ways in which the teen can earn more computer time, such as spending equal time with a younger sibling or joining an after-school club or sports league.

If your teen is working a part-time job, how many hours per week does it entail? Unless the job income is an economic necessity for the family, no teen should work so many hours that it negatively affects school performance or severely restricts all other social and recreational opportunities. Especially if your teen is working only to earn extra spending money, limit the number of hours he or she can work and be sure the teen enjoys a good balance of activities with family and friends.

Does your child spend hours each week cruising the local shopping mall? Too much time in the mall may only increase a teen's dissatisfaction with what she has and make her more vulnerable to excessive spending or the temptation of shoplifting. So here, too, limits may be needed. You may want to restrict visits to the mall to only those times when your teen needs to make a specific purchase. Make sure you know what, if any, dangers lurk at the local mall (for example, gangs, pimps – see Chapter 10) and educate your child about them.

Encourage your teen to be slightly "counter-pop-cultural."

By this we mean encourage your child to be independent, unique and not a slave to every passing fad. When we hear reports of kids refusing to wear logo clothing, shopping at thrift stores, buying generic products, or even making their own clothes, we applaud these efforts. Any time you catch your teen mocking an ad, criticizing a product, or questioning the latest pop-culture icon, ask him to explain his opinion. What does he think the marketer's message really is? Why is she refusing to "buy in" to the message? Discuss the difference between being a leader and being a follower in many avenues of life. Ask how he thinks he and his friends could demonstrate their "independence" from the "herd mentality" encouraged by marketers.

Discourage your teen from being a walking billboard for corporate marketers, particularly those whose brands and advertising you find offensive. Kids may argue that they have a "right" to wear whatever clothing they desire. Explain that they do have the right to clothing that is appropriate for the season and their age. Your responsibility as a parent is to set limits on what is "appropriate." For example, T-shirts advertising liquor or tobacco brands should be out of bounds for teens. If your teen wants to wear a shirt promoting a musician like Eminem, you could explain your prohibition this way: "The lyrics to his music glorify violence toward women. Your mother (sister, girlfriend, etc.) would be deeply hurt and offended if she thought that represented your attitude as well. That's why this shirt is not one that is appropriate for you to wear."

Make gratitude a core value of your family life.

Take time to stop and count your blessings. In the flood of material possessions that flows through our lives, we too often take them for granted and barely acknowledge them before we move on to wanting the next thing. From now on, when someone receives a gift or you purchase an item that will benefit the family or make life easier, pause and savor the moment. Point out how lucky and grateful you are to be able to buy the things you need. Focus on how the family or individual will benefit rather than how much the item cost or what it looks like. All children should be taught how to express thanks verbally or by sending a note or e-mail to gift givers (including their parents!). Being grateful is an attitude you want your children to carry with them always.

When you get something, give something else away.

Another way to make the acquisition of things more thoughtful is to require family members, at least occasionally, to give away a comparable possession when they get something new. For example, if your daughter gets new clothing for school, have her select items to donate to a local homeless shelter or to Goodwill. Use this process to discuss how we all can contribute to the well being of the greater community.

When tragedy or a natural disaster strikes locally or nationally, many kids deal with their fears by helping victims. Whether it's collecting clothing and blankets, fillings sandbags, helping cleanup efforts, or just donating money, kids can display incredible generosity and concern in these situations. We need to help teens see that such impulses should not just be confined to disasters. People are in need every day. As a family, find at least one way to regularly volunteer service to a charitable, church, or community organization. It's important for kids to be aware of how many people have so much less than they do rather than to always compare themselves to the more affluent. Grateful kids are much happier than envious ones.

Talk *with* your teens, not at them.

Make a real effort to have two-way conversations with your child. Teens will tune you out fast if they think you only talk in order to lecture or nag them. So, ask them questions and then really listen to their answers. If you disagree with them, offer your opinion and explain your reasons for it. While you can't force your teen to hold the same opinions you do, you need to make clear what your values and standards of behavior are. Rebellion is normal in teens, but hopefully they are listening to you, and your guidance will make a difference at important moments in their life. It can be done: In a survey of 1,838 middle and high school students, those who said they talked regularly and openly about important issues with their parents also said they tried to live up to their parents' expectations.[4]

If you want to mediate the influence of marketers in your child's value system, you must be knowledgeable about the marketing and content of today's pop culture. This requires more than just viewing the TV shows your teen watches. If you can't or don't want to listen to hip-hop music, view teen movies, visit teen Web sites and chat rooms, or read teen magazines, you can get information from other adults who do. Watch for articles on teen and pop culture in the lifestyle and entertainment sections of your daily newspaper and national news magazines. Many watchdog groups have Web sites or newsletters that report on fads and cultural trends among teens, review movies and music, and offer suggestions to parents. A list of some of them is provided in the "Resources for Parents" section.

When you come across information (e.g., obscene song lyrics or a new body-piercing fad) that concerns or even shocks you, discuss it with your teen. More than likely, your teen will be aware of it before you are. But now is the time to have a calm, open discussion about how you both view the topic – before it becomes personal. Talking things out upfront may head off confrontations later.

Enlist your teen's grandparents.

Because they usually are not a child's primary disciplinarians, grandparents often have special relationships with kids. Grandparents can tell stories about "the way things were" that fascinate kids rather than turn them off like lectures do. If your child loves and respects his or her grandparents, they can be extremely helpful in advocating values and standards in a non-threatening way.

Don't fall into the "guilt money" trap with your children.

Kids need their parents' time, love, and attention. Don't substitute money or possessions for these precious gifts. That just sends the message that people can be replaced by things. If you feel you're not spending enough time with your kids, do something about it! Rearrange family members' schedules so that you can share at least one meal a day together, or plan a family outing where you let your child choose the activity. Work alongside your daughter as she does her chores or share a weekend jog through the neighborhood with your son. Teens may try to push you away in favor of their peers, but secretly they're watching to see if you still care. They might not admit it, but they'd much rather see you on the sidelines of their soccer game or at the family dinner table, than just handing out cash to them as a way of excusing yourself from being there for them.

Violence in Media and Marketing

In the video game "State of Emergency," players use rocket launchers and other high-powered weapons to battle urban rioters, looters, and street gangs in a series of bloody missions to restore order. A Gamers.com review says, "As you play, limbs fly, heads tumble to the ground, and crimson pools fill the gutters. It's excessive, brutal, and hilarious."

• • •

One of the movie tie-in toys marketed to kids ages 4 and up following the release of "The Incredible Hulk" was a set of huge green plastic fists that kids wear over their hands and forearms. "Smash 'n bash sound effects" were trumpeted on the front of the box while a notice in

121

small letters on the back advised parents that "striking a person, pet or inanimate object" with the hands "could result in serious injury."

• • •

NECA, a toymaker, planned to produce a line of action figures to tie in with the release of Quentin Tarantino's R-rated film "Kill Bill," according to Advertising Age *magazine. The characters feature "limbs that fly off and blood (well, red liquid) that spurts." NECA's CEO Joel Weinshanker says, "We want people to be able to recreate scenes of the movie." He insisted, "They're not made for children."[1] But Tarantino told a reporter, "If you are a 12- or 13-year-old, you must go and see 'Kill Bill,' and you will have a damn good time."[2]*

• • •

"Hey victim, should I black your eyes again?

Hey victim, you were the one who put the stick in my hand

I am the ism, my hate's a prism

Let's just kill everyone and let your god sort them out F--- it"

Lyrics to "Irresponsible Hate Anthem," by Marilyn Manson

• • •

It comes as no surprise to most parents that much of the entertainment being marketed to kids includes violence that is increasingly graphic, sexual, and sadistic. Studies have found high levels of profanity, violence, and sexualized violence in all forms of entertainment. Surveys also find parents more and more worried about the coarsening pop culture surrounding their children as well as their ability to shield kids from it. Following is just a sampling of what researchers have found that should concern us all:

- Movies average about 46 violent acts per film, 60 percent of them serious acts, according to a study by the Center for Media and Public Affairs (CMPA).

- While another CMPA study found that the amount of violent content on network TV decreased 11 percent between 1999 and 2001, it also measured a 20 percent increase in violence on basic cable during that time period. A Canadian study found the incidence of physical violence on television increased 378 percent between 1993 and 2001.[3]

- A study funded by the National Cable Television Association found that 57 percent of TV programs contained violence; perpetrators of violent acts went unpunished 73 percent of the time; 47 percent of the violence presented no harm to the victims and 58 percent depicted no pain; 40 percent of the violence included humor; only four percent of violent programs showed nonviolent alternatives to solving problems.

- A 1999 study on the use of profanity in entertainment media revealed that profane language was used once every six minutes on broadcast and cable TV, once every three minutes in films and music videos, and once every two minutes on premium cable shows. In only three percent of instances where profanity was used did viewers hear such terminology condemned or criticized.[4]

Ratings: Help or Hindrance

Alarm over and criticism of violence being marketed to kids is nothing new. Over the years, citizen groups and government panels have prompted the entertainment industries to create and use voluntary ratings systems and warning labels to assist parents in screening for violent content. The ratings systems have multiple problems, however. For example, ratings categories vary among the different entertainment formats. Some tell parents only what age group the entertainment is suitable for, while others also indicate what kind of content is included (violence, nudity, sexual situations, etc.).

Surveys have shown that while a majority of parents use the various ratings systems for information, fewer

The use of **foul language** during the "family viewing hour (8-9 p.m. Eastern time) increased almost **95%** between 1998 and 2002 on the ABC, CBS, NBC, Fox, WB, and UPN networks.

Source: Parents Television Council study, released September 22, 2003

find them helpful. One of the reasons for this may be the phenomenon of "ratings creep." Many perceive that the boundaries of what is acceptable within the ratings categories have been stretched over time. For example, Jay Landers, a former member of the Motion Picture Association of America (MPAA) ratings board, revealed that filmmakers can sometimes "wear down the board" by repeatedly submitting newly edited versions of a film. "Once you see something five or six times," he said, "you can feel, well, maybe they've done enough."[5]

The most discouraging aspect of ratings systems and warning labels, however, is their "forbidden fruit" effect – they can actually entice the audience they are meant to protect. Several studies have found that movie ratings of PG-13 and R increased the desire of young people, especially boys, to view the film. Researchers have found the same correlation between age-based ratings for TV programs and children's desire to watch the shows.[6]

Marketing Violent Entertainment

In September 2000, the Federal Trade Commission released a report that castigated the entertainment industry for specifically targeting children under 17 in marketing campaigns for films, music, and games the industry had labeled as suitable only for adults. The Commission's findings included the following:

- Marketing plans for 80 percent of 44 movies rated R were aimed at children.

- Of 55 music recordings with explicit content labels, all marketing plans expressly targeted those under 17.

- Seventy percent of the 118 electronic games with a Mature rating for violence either targeted children in their marketing plans or were advertised in magazines or TV shows with a large under-17 audience.[7]

A year later, the FTC issued a follow-up report in which it said the movie and electronic game industries had made what it called "commendable progress in limiting their advertising to children of R-rated movies and M-rated games and in providing rating information in advertising." We question the FTC's characterization of the progress made as "commendable." For example, the report noted that film studios were still advertising R-rated movies on television programs favored by teens. And violent games were still being advertised in youth-oriented magazines and popular teen Web sites. Worst of all, the music industry was still marketing "explicit content recordings in most popular teen venues in all media."[8]

The FTC also found in an undercover shopper survey that there had been almost no reduction in the availability of these products being sold to teens. Nearly half of the theaters were still selling tickets to R-rated movies to underage viewers, and 90 percent of the music retailers were selling labeled recordings to underage shoppers. The number of electronic game retailers that were selling to minors decreased, but only from 85 percent to 78 percent.

Clearly, producers and retailers have little or no interest in seeing children and teens restricted from gaining access to violent forms of entertainment. That leaves parents to assume the responsibility. Let's first examine the current state of violence in pop entertainment, and then look at the documented effects that viewing violence has on children.

The Power of 'PG-13'

In 1999, eight of the 20 top-grossing films in the U.S. were rated PG-13 while seven were rated R. By 2002, 13 of the top-grossing films were rated PG-13 and none were rated R. In that same year, PG-13 movies made $4.5 billion while R films made only $2 billion.[9] What explains this dramatic shift? Studios have found that the coveted teen audience flocks to PG-13 action movies but avoids films that are rated G and PG. Teens also have a more difficult time getting into R-rated movies because of parental and theater restrictions. In addition, more parents seem willing to take younger children to PG-13 films, especially those movies featuring cartoon figures that are familiar to children, such as Spider-Man or the Incredible Hulk.

73% of parents feel that limiting children's exposure to popular culture is "nearly **impossible.**"

Source: USA Today/CNN/ Gallup poll, 1998

"Industry watchers say Hollywood moviemakers are pulling out all the stops to shoehorn films into the PG-13 category – and they're doing it from both ends of the ratings spectrum," according to Russ Britt of *CBS Marketwatch*. "Although studios will edit a potentially offensive scene or profanity to change an R into a PG-13, there also are concerns that studios will spice up a movie to bump it up from PG status."[10] Says film critic Roger Ebert, "Movies that ought to be R are being squeezed down into PG-13 in a cynical attempt to increase the potential audience."[11]

The MPAA ratings board has traditionally been more cautious when it comes to sexual content in films, so what usually "spices" a film from PG to PG-13 is violence and/or profanity. In 2003, for the first time ever, family-friendly Walt Disney Pictures released a PG-13 film, "Pirates of the Caribbean." The movie contains a bloody stabbing and computer-generated scenes of moonlight melting the flesh of pirates, transforming them into skeletons.

The *Los Angeles Times* reports, "Industry experts see Disney's decision to release a PG-13 movie under its legendary family film banner as recognition of the chang-

In 2001, only a quarter of the most violent television shows, and two-fifths of the most violent movies, were rated R. The majority were rated PG or PG-13.

Source: Center for Media and Public Affairs

ing cultural, technological and box-office realities that influence today's action-movie market. ... Today, ... youngsters are raised in a more amped-up culture, weaned on violent video games and hyper-realistic visual effects on the Internet and on the big screen."[12]

With producers ratcheting up the violence in PG-13-rated fare like "Spider-Man," "2 Fast 2 Furious," "Lord of the Rings," and "X-Men," parents need to be more aware than ever of movie content in order to monitor and guide their children's viewing choices. It's not enough to be guided solely by ratings. Indeed, in a poll sponsored by CommonSenseMedia.org, only 21 percent of parents said they "completely trust" the movie ratings system. Two of the PG-13 films most often cited by critics of the ratings systems are "The Fast and the Furious" and "2 Fast 2 Furious." The films, according to *USA Today*, "glamorize illegal street racing and other criminal activity and include sex, violence and drunkenness, but they escape the R by avoiding nudity and blood. They have been blamed for the deaths of street-racing teenagers."[13]

Music and Mayhem

American teenagers listen to an estimated 10,500 hours of rock music between seventh and twelfth grades alone – just 500 hours less than they spend in school over 12 years. In 2003, one of the most popular musicians they were listening to was Curtis Jackson, known as 50 Cent. The rapper was born in Queens, New York, to an unmarried 15-year-old who sold crack and was murdered eight years after his birth. 50 Cent was dealing crack himself by the time he was 12, became head of his local drug cartel, and served three years in prison before landing a recording contract in 1997. Ambushed in May 2000, he was shot nine times. He's also been arrested for having two loaded guns in a rented car.[14] Despite, or more likely, because of his violent background, 50 Cent's debut CD, "Get Rich or Die Tryin'," has sold more than five million copies. He also signed a deal with Reebok for a signature footwear collection.[15]

In his song, "What Up Gangsta?," 50 Cent boasts, "I'll have your mama picking out your casket, bastard." Other lyrics in the song include:

*"They say I walk around like got an 'S' on
my chest*

Naw, that's a semi-auto, and a vest on my chest

*I try not to say nothing, the DA might want to
play in court*

But I'll hunt or duck a nigga down like it's sport

Front on me, I'll cut ya, gun-butt or bump ya

*You getting money? I can't none with ya then
f--- ya"*

In today's hip-hop music scene, 50 Cent's violent life is seen as valuable street credibility. He's just the latest in a line of artists like N.W.A., Tupac, Jay-Z, and Ja Rule, who "have made the thug life the predominant theme in hip hop over the past dozen years," says Steve Jones in

USA Today. "Songs flaunting ostentatious wealth and street violence have provided the soundtrack for a generation. Why has gangsta rap remained wildly popular with inner-city, suburban and rural fans alike for so long? Stars such as 50 Cent give fans a window into a life they'll probably never know, a vicarious walk on the wild side, and a chance to be down with what's cool, to 'keep it real.'"[16]

The PBS "Frontline" show titled "The Merchants of Cool" looked at the rise of "rage rock." According to Frontline correspondent Douglas Rushkoff, when MTV saw its ratings start to slide, it embarked on a major research study of teens. One of the "stock characters" to emerge from this study was the "mook," "the perpetual adolescent: crude, misogynistic – and very, very angry." MTV began marketing programs such as "Jackass" and "Spring Break" and music by Limp Bizkit and Eminem to appeal to this teen consumer. Says Rushkoff, "When asked to describe what appeals to them about such music, teens invariably respond that it belongs to them; it hasn't yet been taken and sold back to them at the mall. Full of profanity, violence, and misogyny, rage rock is literally a challenge thrown up to marketers: just try to market this!"[17] Of course, the irony is that rage rock and hip hop are now big business, propelled into the mainstream by the relentless marketing of MTV and the music industry. Hip hop is now the fastest growing radio format, played on more than 150 stations. More than 84 million hip-hop records were sold in 2002.[18]

"Kids' culture and media culture are now one and the same," says Rushkoff, "and it becomes impossible to tell which came first – the anger or the marketing of anger."[19] Whatever the cause, parents are now left to deal with the result – music that pushes unhealthy buttons in teens. For example, in his song "My Name Is," Eminem rages, "I don't give a f---, God sent me to piss the world off." Insane Clown Posse sings, "If I only could, I'd set the world on fire. F--- the world! F--- them all! Don't bother trying to analyze these rhymes, in this song I say f--- 93 times." Snoop Dogg tells us, "You don't like how I'm living, well f--- you."

Violence against women is a dominant theme in the music. Eminem, honored with a Grammy award, has rapped about his sister being gang-raped and raping and murdering his own mother and his wife. The Offspring, in their song "Beheaded," rhyme, "Watch my girlfriend come through the door, Chop off her head, she falls to

"Don't you get it bitch? No one can hear you.

Now shut the f--- up, and get what's comin' to you . . .

You were supposed to love me!!! (sound of Kim choking)

Now bleed, bitch, bleed

Bleed, bitch, bleed, bleeeeed!"

Source: Lyrics from the song "Kim," by Eminem

the floor, Watching my baby's jugular flow, Really makes my motor go."

The bad-boy images, the violent and obscene lyrics, as well as the distinctive street apparel of hip-hop music appeal to both city and suburban teen boys who see wearing the same type of clothing as a sign of rebelliousness and a way to look cool. Bakari Kitwana, author of *Why White Kids Love Hip Hop,* says, "Many white kids feel as locked out of the mainstream as black kids. They want to get away from bland and boring American mainstream culture."[20] The result is an explosion of urban-inspired fashion that has invaded department stores from Macy's to Sears.

The violent imagery in the music and the promotion by gangsta rap artists of certain products like athletic shoes has lead to some questionable marketing ploys. Converse, the company that invented basketball shoes but which has seen shrinking sales in recent years, announced plans to launch a new shoe to go by the name "Loaded Weapon" and to be endorsed and advertised by five NBA rookies. A Converse marketer claimed, "It's just a shoe we're talking about. I don't think there'll be any confusion that this refers to anything other than an athletic shoe." But the shoe launch drew immediate criticism from Jim Hainey, executive director of the National Association of Basketball Coaches, who said, "My immediate reaction is that it sickens me, especially in the wake of (slain Baylor basketball player) Patrick Dennehy. This hits me in the gut."[21]

The murder of Run-DMC member Jason Mizell (Jam Master Jay) didn't stop Dr Pepper from airing a commercial featuring the hip-hop group that was filmed before his death. John Clarke, chief advertising officer of Dr Pepper/7 UP called the ad "a fitting tribute" to the rapper. "Like Dr Pepper, Run-DMC and Jason Mizell were one-of-a-kind," he said in a publicity release posted on the company's Web site.[22]

Though there is yet no sign of that hip hop's popularity is waning, some within the industry are starting to question the music's glorification of negative and criminal behavior. Chuck D, formerly of Public Enemy, says "The illusion of thug and gangster is almost a romantic thing. But at the end of the day, thug and gangster only feeds two other cottage industries: death and jail. We have the largest black population ever in jail right now."[23]

Adrian Arceo, a writer for the Web site Allhiphop.com, claims that hip-hop music originally was "all about positivity and having fun. ... Today the hip hop scene is almost the complete opposite. Artists are claiming to be thugs and gangsters; disrespecting women, glorifying violence, and promoting drug use in their lyrics and videos. This trend has led to too much media glamorization of thugs and gangsters in hip-hop music. ... The mainstream audience labels music with positive messages as not 'real' when in fact the thug image is what is not real."[24] Arceo reports that a number of rappers are struggling to reverse the trend. For example, Gift of Gab, in his song "Shallow Days," sings:

One-quarter to one-third of young male felons imprisoned for committing violent crimes like homicide, rape, and assault, report having consciously **imitated** crime techniques they **watched on TV.**

Source: Brandon Centerwall, "Studies in Violence and Television,"
Journal of American Medical Association

"*But music does reflect life and kids look up to what you're portraying and mimic what you act like.*

It's time for a new day an era in rap, conscious styles, makin' them aware of the happenings.

But their ears seem more steered towards self-annihilation so then they might laugh and write us off,

Like I'm out here just blowing wind, maybe they label us soft or unreal, something they can't feel,

While they keep yelling murder, murder, murder, kill, kill, kill."

Sway Calloway, who interviewed 50 Cent for an MTV special, reflected afterward, "It's funny to me how everybody from the streets to the suburbs to the corporate world are embracing America's black sheep, overlooking his murderous lyrics, his tales of drug trade, misogyny, and so forth. ... It is so typical for 'pop culture' to latch onto something that it doesn't really understand in order to appear hip, only to abandon it when the reality extends to the malls, the workplace, and the bedrooms of its children. The industry exploits a dysfunctional community and consumers fantasize about it and buy it. What about working toward healing it?"[25]

Playing Violent Games

Electronic gaming has exploded as a source of entertainment for American children. On *average,* Americans spent 75 hours each in 2003 playing video games, double the amount of time spent in 1997.[26] There is a whole subculture or cyber-community of gamers, however, who put those numbers to shame. Jonathan Wendel, for example, a three-time world champion, admits to spending *40 hours a week* honing his gaming skills. When he was a teen, he says, "my parents hated me playing video games all the time. They grounded me constantly."[27] A study by the Pew Internet & American Life Project found that 100 percent of the college students they polled said they had played video games. "Gaming is a part of growing up in the U.S.," its report concluded.

What worries many parents is the type of games that kids are playing. A Senate Judiciary Committee report stated that only two percent of kids surveyed said they played "education games." Instead, the vast majority said they preferred to play ultra-violent games like "Doom" and "Mortal Kombat." Thirty percent of all video games advertised during TV's "family hour" were rated M (the equivalent of an R movie rating), according to a Parents Television Council study. At a 2003 game-fest sponsored by id Software, maker of violent games like "Doom" and "Quake," families, couples, and mothers with kids showed up to play computer death matches with top game players.[28]

Here are some examples of the content of best-selling games:

- In "Grand Theft Auto 3," players carjack and steal drugs from street people and pushers. Players have sex with prostitutes and then beat them to death with baseball bats.

- In "Carmeggedon," players earn points for mowing down pedestrians to the sound of breaking bones.

- In "Duke Nukem," players hone their shooting skills by using pornographic posters of women for target practice. They get bonus points for shooting naked and bound prostitutes and strippers who beg, "Kill me."

- In "Postal," players act the part of a Postal Dude who randomly shoots everyone who appears, including people walking out of church and members of a high school band. Postal Dude is programmed to say, "Only my gun understands me."

"Video game violence is now an epidemic," says Dr. David Walsh, president of the National Institute on Media and the Family. The organization gave the industry an F for social responsibility in its "MediaWise Video

Game Report Card." "Violence against women has become a black mark on the entire industry. This failing grade is a wake-up call for everyone: manufacturers, retailers and parents, Walsh says."[29]

As the first generation of video gamers has grown into young adulthood, the blood and gore has intensified to the point that the Entertainment Software Ratings Board has expanded the "descriptors," or phrases, it uses to indicate the violent content in the games it rates. In addition to existing descriptors – animated blood, blood and gore, comic mischief (gross humor), suggestive or mature sexual themes, and violence – the board has added these labels:

- Cartoon violence. Cartoonish characters get hurt but may be unharmed afterwards.

- Fantasy violence. Human or non-human character violence, easily distinguishable from reality.

- Intense violence. Graphic and realistic physical conflict with blood, gore, weapons, injury, or death.

- Sexual violence. Depictions of rape or other violent sexual acts.

According to the ratings board, the gaming public has matured – the average age is 28 – along with the subject matter. Ratings Board president Patricia Vance warns, "When parents pick up a popular game that has an M on it, they need to know it isn't meant for teens, that it really is for ages 17 and over."[30]

Effects of Violent Entertainment

A long and substantial body of laboratory research has documented the impact on children of viewing televised violence. The American Psychological Association says the three major effects are these:

- Children may become less sensitive to the pain and suffering of others.

- Children may be more fearful of the world around them.

- Children may be more likely to behave in aggressive or harmful ways toward others.[31]

Real-life studies have revealed the long-range effects of watching televised violence. Leonard Eron, Ph.D., found that elementary school kids who watched a lot of violence showed higher levels of aggression when they were teens. At age 30, the same individuals were also more likely to be arrested and prosecuted for criminal acts.[32]

The "negative and destructive themes" in much of today's popular music and music videos have been identified as a concern by the American Academy of Child

60% of parents believe "negative role models in society" are a major cause of **rude** and **disrespectful** behavior by children.

Source: "Aggravating Circumstances" poll, 2002, Public Agenda and Adolescent Psychiatry (AACAP). The organization listed these themes as prominent in today's music:

- Advocating and glamorizing abuse of drugs and alcohol

- Pictures and explicit lyrics presenting suicide as an "alternative" or "solution"

- Graphic violence

- Rituals in concerts

- Sex that focuses on control, sadism, masochism, incest, children, devaluing women, and violence toward women.

AACAP says that music "is not usually a danger" for a teen whose life is "happy and healthy." But it warns parents to watch for teens who are "persistently preoccupied with music that has seriously destructive themes" and whose behavior changes to include things such as isolation, depression, alcohol or other drug abuse."[33] These teens may need professional help.

Research on the effects of violent video gaming is just getting under way, but some disturbing results are already being seen. Fred Guterl of *Newsweek International*

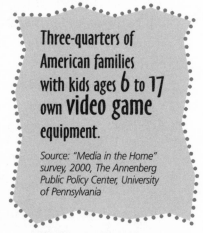

Three-quarters of American families with kids ages 6 to 17 own video game equipment.

Source: "Media in the Home" survey, 2000, The Annenberg Public Policy Center, University of Pennsylvania

looked at the studies to date and reported, "From the brain's point of view, gaming is largely a visual task, and as such it gets processed mainly in the right hemisphere. What worries scientists is that the right-lobe visual circuits have a fast track to the emotions. If you read about a violent event, the information is filtered through your more rational, analytical left hemisphere. Richard Restak, a neurologist at George Washington University and the author of *The New Brain,* argues that visual media like video games and television don't get tempered in this way.

"According to a study by psychologist Craig Anderson of the University of Missouri-Columbia, an overload of emotion-charged imagery can increase anti-social behavior. In a study of college students published in 2000 in the *Journal of Personality and Social Psychology,* he found that playing violent games like 'Mortal Kombat' correlated strongly to aggressive personalities, poor academic performance and delinquency."[34]

Messages that many violent video games send to kids are:

- Problems can be resolved quickly and with little interest.

- The best way to solve a problem is to eliminate the source of the problem.

- Problems are right or wrong, black or white.

- It is acceptable to immerse oneself in the video game's rule-driven reality without questioning the rules.

- Use instinctual rather than thoughtful, responsible behaviors to react to problems.

- Personal imagination is not an important problem-solving skill.[35]

The evidence exists that violence in TV, films, music, and video games can be damaging to kids. What can parents do to protect children from the onslaught of violent media? We have suggestions for you in Chapter 11.

Sex Sells

A four-story tall image of Jenna Jameson, X-rated porn star, adorns a billboard in New York City's Times Square. A nude Jameson is interviewed in the shower about her "preparations" for the Cannes Film Festival by a reporter from E! Entertainment Television holding a strategically placed microphone.

• • •

"In (the PG-13 rated film) 'Charlie's Angels: Full Throttle,' Demi Moore lasciviously licks Cameron Diaz's face, the Angels bump and grind in a production number, and numerous double-entendres refer to group sex and hookers," reports USA Today.[1]

• • •

To market their CDs, female pop stars are showing more and more skin. Christina Aguilera posed nude with only her guitar as a cover-up for Rolling Stone *magazine; Mariah Carey took a skinny dip in her bathtub during MTV's visit to her home; Mya wore sheer short shorts in soft porn poses for* King *magazine.*

• • •

It's a cliché: Sex sells, at least marketers believe that it does. Sexual innuendo has long been a part of advertising and marketing directed at adults. What's different today is how graphic sexuality is being used to market products and entertainment to teenage-and-younger boys and girls. In most cases, the sexual humor is crude; the sex is casual, devoid of emotion, and without consequences; and women are often depicted as victims of horrific violence. Sexual images and references are so pervasive in marketing and the media that children mimic behavior they are too young to understand: A five-year-old girl, trying on clothing in a department store, pirouetted in front of her mother and asked, "Do I look sexy?"

After MTV undertook its exhaustive study of American teens in the late 1990s, it began marketing "stock characters" to American teens. As we discussed in the last chapter, teen boys are characterized as "mooks," defined as infantile, angry, female-hating boors. Teen girls, labeled "midriffs," are portrayed as highly sexualized, world-weary sophisticates.[2] This "midriff" type glowers out at young girls from billboards and the pages of teen magazines and populates TV shows such as

"Dawson's Creek" and movies like "Cruel Intentions." The type also cavorts through the raunchy teen movies marketed to adolescent boys, and female artists emulate the image in music videos and on CD covers to sell to the same audience.

It's no surprise that the self-esteem of young girls "plummets" when they reach adolescence or that one in five girls has an eating disorder, says advertising critic and lecturer Jean Kilbourne. Advertising tells girls that only the ideal image is acceptable – thin, tall, long legged, broad shouldered, and large breasted – a body type that is genetically rare or achieved by implants, by plastic surgery, or by retouching photos on the computer. Girls learn that their bodies will be routinely scrutinized and criticized. In ads, women's bodies are turned into objects, "dismembered" into body parts, and often portrayed in passive poses, according to Kilbourne.[3]

In addition, ads and the mass media carry disturbing messages about sex to both girls and boys. In the media, sex is divorced from relationships, intimacy, emotions, morals, and values; sex is trivialized to sell products. Especially damaging is violence portrayed as eroticism. Teens may argue that they are wise to the advertisers' crass intent to sell. But advertising helps to shape our view of the world; it sells us not only products but attitudes and values as well. It also heavily influences the content of the media that carry the ads.

'Teen' Magazines

According to the 2000 U.S. Census, the population of girls between the ages of 15 and 19 was projected to jump by 18 percent between 1992 and 2005. One industry to benefit from this is the teen-girl category of magazine publishing. The category is ruled by six major titles, according to *Advertising Age: Seventeen, Teen, YM, CosmoGirl, Teen Vogue,* and *Elle Girl.*[4] Although each title has its own focus (fashion, celebrities, music, etc.), the overriding message in all six is that teen girls are obsessed with looks, shopping, and boys. While some of the stories hyped on October 2003 magazine covers ("Get great style – on a budget" or "4 ways to find your next boyfriend") seem time-warped from the 1950s, others are a sad or silly commentary on our times ("I was a teen prostitute," "A cute butt in 3 weeks," and "Paris Hilton on what it's like to be filthy rich"). Inside the magazines, it's easy to confuse the consumer-oriented

Teen Girl Magazines $

Total ad spending in 2002	$345.8 million
Total circulation in 2002	7,700,000
U.S. population, girls 15-19	9,828,886

Sources: TNS Media Intelligence/CMR, Audit Bureau of Circulations, 2000 U.S. Census

editorial content with the advertising. The magazines are little more than catalogs filled with products, and the "sell" is relentless. Page after page hypes new clothing, accessories, and makeup; photos of celebrities come with prices and retail sources for the clothing they're wearing. In a cover story of Michelle Branch, a rock star known for her covered-up jeans and T-shirt style on stage, *Elle Girl* highlights this quote from her: "I'm starting to get into clothes more and actually wanting to look a little sexy."[5] (The magazine apparently doesn't want its readers to think fashion and looking sexy aren't important!)

The ads inside these teen magazines (read by a large audience of preteen girls) often use models who are considerably older than their target audience, and many feature blatantly sexual images or racy ad copy. Here are a few typical examples from *Seventeen,* "America's most-read young women's magazine":

- The body of a bikini-clad woman (the photo ends at the neck) with the advertising line: "One more reason to get it on."

- "Scent to bed – FCUK fragrance" printed over a photo of a boy and girl, snuggled in bed together, in their underwear.

- "Feel the love" with Wetslicks lipstick.

- A mascara brush posed next to an impossibly high stiletto-heeled shoe.

- "American Idol" winner Kelly Clarkson wearing Candies boots but otherwise nude in a bubble bath.

Even the names of the clothing lines and companies marketed to teen girls can be disturbing; for example, Hot Kiss, Dollhouse, and Killah ("Lolita with a rock 'n' roll street edge!").

"Lolita" seems to be the operative image these magazines push to their adolescent readers. Mixed in with the fashion and skin care advice and a few features on "real teens," the magazines offer editorial content such as:

- A rundown of new "gotta see" TV shows that includes "Coupling," whose plot is described as "six sex-crazed friends swap sordid stories – and one another's bedmates."[6]

- A fictional short story that opens in a 16-year-old girl's bedroom just after she's had sex with her boyfriend. The couple's relationship is portrayed as "true love" despite their ages and the fact that he is bipolar and suffers from fits of weeping and rage. Their parents are variously described as "detached," "stony," and "clueless."[7]

- A list of "girls gone wild" – young actresses who've gone from starring in "fluff" movies to roles like "the girlfriend of porn star and murder suspect John Holmes" in the R-rated film "Wonderland."[8]

- An "Answer Guy" columnist who responds to a reader's question, "I'm 16, how old a guy do you think it's okay for me to date," by saying there's a "significant problem" with dating a guy over 18 because "if you're sexually active, some states say minors aren't old enough to make their own decisions about sex, so you could tell him you want to have sex and really mean it, but the law might automatically consider it statutory rape."[9]

- A "Dating World" column, in which the female author gives this tip: "During some thorough fieldwork, I realized that boys pretty much always put out in a photo booth (it's like a grown girl's ticket to five minutes in a broom closet)."[10]

Television

The ad for Dr Pepper looks like an MTV music video: Singer Anastacia and a bevy of backup dancers, showing plenty of cleavage, bare midriffs, and wearing short shorts, grind their hips and shake other body parts for the camera. A Miller Lite commercial shows two well-endowed young women in a cement-wrestling, torn-clothing fight over whether the beer "tastes great" or is "less filling." During the 1999 Super Bowl, Victoria's Secret paraded models in bras and panties across the screen for 30 seconds and sent more than a million viewers scurrying to their computers to log on to the company's Web site for a better look.[11]

Young teens (ages 13-15) rank **entertainment** media as the **top source** of information about sexuality and sexual health.

Source: Mediascope, March 15, 2000

No matter how closely you screen your child's TV viewing habits, it's virtually impossible to avoid having kids exposed to commercials like these when they pop up on sitcoms and sporting events.

Ads, like program content, have become more and more graphic as broadcast networks and basic cable channels struggle to keep from losing more of their audiences to each other and to the sexually explicit premium cable channels. Audiences are what TV programmers sell to advertisers, and if there aren't enough viewers or the "right kind" of viewers, programs don't survive. For example, the family program "Dr. Quinn, Medicine Woman" was number one in its time slot but was canceled because its audience wasn't young or rich enough to command the high advertising rates the network wanted to charge.[12] What have the networks and basic cable found that pulls those desirable viewers in? Sitcoms with lots of sexual innuendo ("Friends") and smart-mouth kids ("That '70s Show," "South Park"), reality shows that titillate with their outrageous sexual situations ("Joe Millionaire," "The Bachelor") or disgust with revolting stunts ("Fear Factor"), and dramas that constantly push the boundaries of what can be shown on prime time (beginning years ago with a glimpse of Dennis Franz's bare backside in "NYPD Blue" and progressing to scenes of sexual intercourse in "Nip/Tuck").

A study of the broadcast networks from 1998 to 2002 by the Parents Television Council (PTC) suggested that while the trend toward sexual content was slowing on some channels, the content itself was growing more explicit. The PTC said its study found that the amount of sexual content on TV during the "family hour" (8-9 p.m. Eastern time) had dropped on ABC, CBS, Fox, NBC, and UPN. (Only on the WB network had sexual content increased over that time span, but the rise was a whopping 87.6 percent.) Offsetting the overall decrease, however, was the "coarsening of content." According to the PTC study, "in 1998, non-marital sex, references to prostitution, transvestites, adultery, nudity and pornography accounted for less than 3 percent of all sexual content. In 2002, such material accounted for 26 percent of all sexual content."

During the same year, a Kaiser Family Foundation survey found that two-thirds of all television shows have some sexual content. Kids can see a lot of it just surfing through network and basic cable channels. Here's what we've stumbled across just changing channels during evening prime time:

- An "E! True Hollywood Story" about porn star Jenna Jameson that featured her talking about various sexual encounters, including one with rock star Marilyn Manson.

- An episode of "South Park" where one of the cartoon youngsters follows his father to a bathhouse where he sees him having gay sex.

- A stunt on Spike TV's pseudo-reality program "The Joe Schmo Show" where contestants licked a chocolate-covered, nearly nude woman to reveal clues painted on her body.

- Tipsy coeds participating in a wet T-shirt contest in a bar full of rowdy college students.

When asked by a news reporter how much sexual content on TV was too much, Peter Liguori, president of FX network, replied, "As a programmer, we're all mindful that there are, and should be, limits."[13] It's hard to imagine what those limits might be considering Liguori's network is responsible for some of the raciest fare on the tube, including "Nip/Tuck" and "The Shield." Another executive, Martin D. Franks, CBS executive vice president in charge of standards, commented, "The culture changes. ... I don't know whether we lead the culture or reflect it. I think we reflect it."[14] Yet Kaiser Family Foundation researchers make this observation: "If you ask teens what role sex on TV plays in their own lives, nearly three out of four say it influences the sexual behaviors of youngsters their age and one in four admits it influences their own behavior."[15]

In light of research like this, it's appalling that any advertiser would choose to associate itself with programs like those described above. But although there are conservative advertisers that maintain lists of shows they avoid, ad agency executive Catherine Warburton-Scott says, "If a show is successful, most clients bend the rules a little bit in terms of content. They are willing to compromise on content if the program has high ratings and a good buzz."[16] What does it say about our culture when marketers and the entertainment industry place high ratings and a good buzz ahead of the welfare of our children?

Music Videos, Lyrics, and Marketing

In hip-hop music videos it's not uncommon to see scores of scantily clad women reduced to nothing more than body parts as they gyrate around the male rappers. MTV produced a show on sex in music videos that had an entire segment devoted to the "booty" shots that dominate these videos. Women are merely sexual objects in these videos,

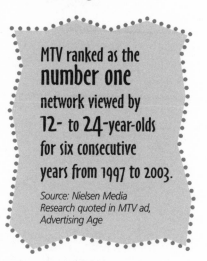

MTV ranked as the **number one** network viewed by 12- to 24-year-olds for six consecutive years from 1997 to 2003.

Source: Nielsen Media Research quoted in MTV ad, Advertising Age

bumping and grinding their torsos, often without their faces ever being shown. In the lyrics, women are often referred to as "bitches" or "hoes," and pimping is glorified. Consider these lyrics:

> *"I holla at a ho til I got a bitch confused*
>
> *She got on Payless, me I got on gator shoes*
>
> *I'm shopping for chinchillas, in the summer they cheaper*
>
> *Man this ho you can have her, when I'm done I ain't gon keep her*
>
> *Man, bitches come and go, every nigga pimpin know"*
>
> – 50 Cent in "P.I.M.P."

*"It's getting hot in herre (so hot), so take off all
    your clothes*

*I am – getting so hot, I wanna take my
    clothes off*

Uh, uh, uh – let it hang all out!
    – Nelly in "Hot in Herre"

"I remember the first time I had a taste

She pulled her panties down

And shoved her Cotton in my face

I said 'Your daddy's home'

She said 'So f---in what'"
    – Insane Clown Posse in "Cotton Candy"

In too many of these songs, women are just com-
modities to be used, abused, even sold, and then discarded. The women are also portrayed as grasping and
greedy: "She dancing for dollars, She got a thing for that
Gucci, that Fendi, that Prada" (50 Cent in "P.I.M.P.").

The glorification of pimping is another sad byprod-
uct of songs by rappers like Nelly and 50 Cent. Nelly has
launched a caffeine-packed energy drink called Pimp
Juice. (Similar nonalcoholic, hip-hop-related drinks are
popular in nightclubs as vodka mixers.) The marketer of
the beverage, Demetrius Denham of Fillmore St.
Brewery, insists that the word "pimp" has taken on a
new meaning, saying, "This word means more – like
your charisma. It's what gives you that extra edge."

Many people don't buy that explanation and contend the name is an insult to women. Black activist groups such as the Black Anti-Defamation League have urged consumers to boycott the drink. Predictably, the controversy has spurred sales of Pimp Juice. "Every time somebody says something negative about it, it brings our sales up," claimed Denham.[17] An executive of the 7-Eleven chain stores, which are considering selling Pimp Juice, said, "You can't underestimate the bottom line here. The opportunity is terrific."[18]

Unfortunately, the bared skin, dirty dancing, and explicit lyrics of hip hop have also spread to the marketing and music of more and more young female pop stars who have shed their clothes to boost media attention and sales of their CDs. Beyonce, Britney Spears, Christina Aguilera, Jewel, Mya, and Ashanti Douglas are just some of the artists who have shown up in various states of undress on CD and magazine covers, in music videos, and at music award shows. There's more than just a hint of desperation to it as the music industry scrambles for a way to reverse declining sales.

One study found that 75% of all music videos that told a story involved sexual imagery and more than half involved **violence**, usually against **women**.

Source: Pediatrics, January 2001

(Madonna, victim of slipping sales, shared a salacious kiss with Spears on MTV's Music Awards program and showed up all over the media for days afterward.) In a backwards spin on feminism, the raunchy behavior is defended as women asserting their "independence" or battling a "double standard" that "allows men to exhibit their bodies but considers the women who do it sluts." But it's hard to see "liberation" when it's women who are voicing lyrics like the following:

> *"I dipped it and I stripped it and I ripped it like before*
>
> *I had her screamin', nope no diddily, nope no more*
>
> *I can't stop once I get started*
>
> *But yo honey, uh, get them legs parted"*
>
>   – Madonna in "Erotica"

> *"Oh pretty babe, I shouldn't have let you go*
>
> *I must confess that my loneliness*
>
> *Is killin me now*
>
> *Don't you know I still believe*
>
> *That you will be here*
>
> *And give me a sign, hit me baby one more time"*
>
>   – Britney Spears in "Baby One More Time"

These pop star images, in addition to influencing girls' and teens' clothing styles (see Chapter 5), are even starting to trickle down into the toy market. Tween girls may still collect stuffed animals but toy makers have found their taste in dolls is changing. Mattel has created an edgier look for its My Scene Barbie, and its new hip-hop styled dolls called Flavas wear torn clothing and low-slung wide leg pants and come packaged with their own wall of graffiti. MGA Entertainment is selling pouty-lipped Bratz dolls dressed in sultry fashions.

Pornography in the Mainstream

Another noticeable trend is the movement of adult-film stars into mainstream advertising and media. Pornography used to be restricted to XXX movie theaters, magazines like *Hustler* and *Penthouse,* and under-the-counter videocassette rentals. Now porn stars are showing up everywhere from billboards to network TV to the publishing industry. Motley Crue, Eminem, and others have featured them in music videos; Howard Stern regularly interviews them on his radio show; Jenna Jameson played herself on NBC's "Mister Sterling;" three "Vivid girls" are pictured on Sims snowboards; the pornography business is the central setting for the Fox TV show "Skin," the Showtime reality series "Family Business," and the movies "The People vs. Larry Flynt" and "Wonderland."

More responsible than anything else for the "increased visibility and acceptability" of pornography, according to *Newsweek,* is the Web. "Because of the anonymous nature of Internet surfing, porn sites have proliferated since they first started appearing. ... Analysts estimate that the Web's 100,000 adult pornographic sites now take in $1 billion annually."[19] Porn can invade your home or your teen's computer even when he or she is not looking for it. MSNBC correspondent Lisa Napoli asked kids about their experiences with porn sites on the Internet. They reported coming across them when typing in seemingly innocent Web addresses such as "teenscene." A 15-year-old wrote, "I was looking for pictures of elephants for my aunt and I stumbled upon pictures of women having sex with animals, not a pretty picture." Other teens said that porn "was one of the easiest things to find on the Internet. ... It's simply thinking of a dirty word and adding on '.com' or typing it into (a) search engine."[20] Kids reported they had found ways to get around protective filtering devices installed on school computers. Children can also be exposed to porn marketing via the e-mail spamming that afflicts so many home computers.

On average, children are exposed to more than 14,000 sexual references each year.

Source: American Academy of Pediatrics Media Education Policy Statement, 1999

Today, a lot of corporate America is tied to the adult sex industry: In Hollywood, the adult film industry makes $4 billion on 6,000 movies a year – about as much as National Football League revenues; hotels rent 10 times as many adult films to business travelers as standard movies; telephone companies make money from phone sex operations and soon will distribute adult entertainment over picture phones.[21] What's next? Trend watcher Irma Zandl says strippers are "really setting the trends right now." There already are exercise classes and home videotapes for women that feature stripping. "I think we'll see pole dancing on ESPN in five years," Zandl says.[22]

Teen Web Sites

Kids don't need to visit pornographic Web sites to find a lot of sexual information on the Internet. Many sites that market themselves to teens include graphic or racy content in their chat rooms, advice columns, and resource sections. On the popular gURL.com site, we found these topics addressed in its resource section – abortion, bisexuality, "dry humping," oral sex, orgasms, and birth control – among many other sexually related subjects. All were discussed in a straightforward, but also value-free, way. An advice column was filled with comments like these: "Many people find that they don't always have to be 'dating' or 'in love' with someone in order to share the fun of a sexual experience with them" or "You should never have any kind of sex unless you know for sure that you want to." This site is marketed to girls as young as 13, and there is nothing, other than parental oversight, that prohibits even younger girls from accessing this information.

Another site for teens, Bolt.com tends to let other teens dole out the advice on sexual topics. So in response to a poll on the question, "Would you rather have sex without love or love without sex?," Bolt has teens posting answers such as: "Sex with out (sic) love. Because (sic) doing someone (sic) is so fun and love takes time." The site also offers a "honey search" and ways to meet other members online. It asks for the visitor's age category in ranges from 15-16 to 24 or older, but the anonymity of the Web makes it easy for a visitor to masquerade in any age group and make contact with a much younger or older person.

Web sites like these that are marketed to teens pose many dilemmas for parents. It is difficult to prevent

How an average woman's measurements compare to those of a Barbie doll and a store mannequin:

	Average woman	Barbie	Store mannequin
Height	5' 4"	6' 0"	6' 0"
Weight	145 lbs.	101 lbs	Not available
Dress size	11 – 14	4	6
Bust	36 – 37"	39"	34"
Waist	29 – 31"	19"	23"
Hips	40 – 42"	33"	34"

Source: *Health* magazine, September 1997

young kids from accessing them. Some of them encourage teens to believe that all wisdom resides within themselves, that all they have to do is listen to their peers for the answer to any problem. Others offer information that you may believe your child is too young to have access to or to understand. Much of the content is offered without judgments of any kind regarding moral standards, personal obligations, or social responsibility. To grab teens' attention, the sites exude a "let it all hang out" attitude. The fact that these sites are merely smokescreens to sell more stuff to kids or to collect marketing data on them just makes them more offensive to parents.

Effects of Sexual Advertising and Media on Kids

Reactorz Research polled 200 kids and teens to gauge their reaction to sexually provocative clothing ads on billboards, transit shelters, buses, and in popular magazines. They concluded that to kids between the ages of 8 and 12, the sexual ads had become "background noise – so common that they don't provoke comment or even awareness unless pointed out to them." Teens considered themselves to be very savvy regarding the advertising. According to Reactorz, "They understand sex sells but they don't think that they are influenced by the advertising – they feel they see through it for what it is, a manipulative technique *that works on everyone else.*" The researchers found that teens especially found the ads offensive and wanted the opportunity to discuss the issue with their parents. The teens also wanted to convey to marketers that they felt that sex in advertising was getting too explicit and that they worried over its impact. Unfortunately, the teens in some cases said they admired the clothing "despite" the offensive advertising and also admitted that the advertising might have a long-range impact on their body image and self-esteem.[23]

These kids and teens reflect some of the confusing as well as volatile reactions we have to the onslaught of sexual images sent our way in today's pop culture. They offend many of us, but their sheer number may have also numbed us to their true impact. What are some of the effects these messages have on children?

First, children suffer from a loss of innocence. Parents used to be able to protect children from information they were too young to understand. Society cooperated by limiting sexually explicit information and entertainment to media outlets that could only be easily accessed by adults. This social contract to shield children no longer exists. In the frenetic race to sell things or to capture an audience for marketers, most of the barriers have come tumbling down. Near nudity, sexual situations and innuendo, simulated sexual intercourse – all of it is available in media and advertising readily accessible to children, whether it is intended for them or not. As a result, many kids have acquired a lot of sexual information without much moral, emotional, or spiritual context.

The images of women in advertising and the media have placed young girls at grave risk, both physically and emotionally. On one hand, the "perfect woman" image portrayed in advertising has damaged the self-esteem, body image, and health of young females. The Anorexia Nervosa and Related Eating Disorders organization reports that more than half of teen girls are, or think they should be, on a diet, while three percent go too far and become anorexic or bulimic.[24] (The emphasis on the "buff" male body has correspondingly led to concerns over a rise in eating disorders in and the use of steroids by boys.) Teen girls can also put enormous amounts of money and effort into makeup, hair straightening or dyeing, body piercing, hair removal, and countless other cosmetic efforts (even plastic surgery) to achieve some unreachable ideal image.

On the other hand, the trend toward skin-baring, sexy clothing in ads and on celebrities has led girls to believe that this clothing choice is a "power statement" that has no consequences for them. When teachers in Greenport, New York, confiscated 12 string bikinis from the seniors headed to Florida on a class trip, these were some of the reactions by the girls: "I'm not such a little girl, that I'm unaware of my own body ... and can't make decisions about what is and is not appropriate for me to wear" and "Look at billboards and television and fashion advertising – what are we supposed to look like?"[25] Girls are clearly being put at risk by sexual media messages.

The objectification and debasement of women in ad images and media entertainment negatively affects boys and young men. The parade of women as little more than body parts, the glorification of porn stars as media celebrities, the hip-hop tendency to classify women as either bitches or "hoes," the use of women as targets for horrific violence in video games – all these depictions desensitize boys and degrade their view of women. Many male-female relationships in the media lack the caring emotions of honesty, trust, empathy, respect, or love. Sex is portrayed as just a game in which the "cool" guys try to score as often as they can. When kids admit that their own sexual behavior is influenced by media examples, it's disturbing to wonder what quality of relationships, marriage, and family life will be in store for boys and girls growing up in such a culture.

Who's Raising Your Child?

We'll close this chapter with a frightening example of what has happened to some young girls who've been seduced by materialism and pop culture's casual approach to sex. *Newsweek* reported that law enforcement has seen the following trends in teen prostitution: it is increasing; the kids are getting younger; they are subject to increasing violence from pimps, and while most teen prostitutes are runaways, illegal immigrants, or from poor urban areas, a growing number come from middle-class homes. The prime recruiting areas for pimps are the local shopping malls, and successful recruiting tactics include buying the girls gifts and luring them with thoughts of how much money they can make.

Child advocates, according to *Newsweek,* are especially worried and puzzled by the middle-class girls "who aren't forced into prostitution but instead appear to sell themselves for thrills, or money, or both. Richard Estes, a University of Pennsylvania researcher, says ... he found middle-class teenage girls traveling to Tijuana to make quick money by prostituting themselves to U.S. servicemen. 'We also found identical patterns with kids in the San Francisco Bay Area and in Honolulu.' Estes says his research shows the girls would often invite men to their homes after school, while their parents were still at work."

The magazine interviewed a 17-year-old girl, "Stacey," who said she encountered an older, well-dressed man in a shopping mall who told her how pretty she was and offered to buy her a $250 outfit if she would model the clothes for him. Stacey says she learned from the encounter that "potentially good sex is a small price to pay for the freedom to spend money on what I want." She went on to stripping and then having sex with men in hotel rooms for money that she used to buy clothes.[26]

What lessons are Stacey and other young people learning from our marketing-, sex-, and violence-saturated culture? What lessons is your child learning? Who's raising your child?

Final Thoughts
for Parents

"Advertisers knew that empowered children could make better consumers than dependent, compliant ones, and they were naturally attracted to media content that could advance that cause. One way that the media could hasten the empowerment of children was by reducing authorities, and parents especially, in the child-consumer's eyes," comments Kay Hymowitz in her essay, "The Contradictions of Parenting in a Media Age."[1] How often in popular culture have we seen portrayals of smart, sophisticated, competent children being parented by bumbling dolts?

Here's a scene that advertisers have encouraged and only a marketer could love, and it's probably taken place in your home more than once: An exasperated child rolls his eyes and shakes his head at another "clueless" comment or opinion offered by his "totally out of it" parent. Since the 1950s, childhood has changed: Children today are immersed in the media, in all of its many new forms. They spend less time with their parents and are less subject to the authority of other adults like teachers and neighbors. Says Hymowitz, "This new landscape of childhood means that at a time when work hours are more demanding and when somewhere around a third of all adults rearing children don't have the helping hand of a spouse, parents need to do something they've never been required to do before perhaps at any time in history: deliberately and consciously counter many of the dominant messages of their own culture."[2]

"It's up to the parents to ... " – how many times have we heard marketers, filmmakers, TV producers, singers, actors, etc., absolve themselves of guilt for any harmful effects their product might have on children and point to you as being the one solely responsible for protecting your children. After all, they claim, they have the "right" to make a buck and to express themselves in almost any way they want. Sometimes it's difficult to believe that the people producing much of our current advertising and entertainment are parents themselves. And a substantial number of them may not be. For example, a colleague of ours whose daughter works in the television industry notes that many of those working in the reality TV area are young, single, and childless. On a much broader scale, the proportion of singles in the U.S. population has

tripled since 1940 from eight to 26 percent,[3] snagging the attention of Hollywood and marketers.

The unfortunate fact is that we live in a society whose marketing and entertainment industries have pretty much washed their hands of responsibility for the raising of our children. And many parents are in despair: Almost nine of 10 parents in a USA Today/CNN/Gallup Poll said it was "harder today to raise kids to be 'good people' than it was 20 years ago." Parents said that the time (35-40 hours a week) their kids spent with TV, movies, video and computer games, and videotapes was isolating them and immersing them in sex, violence, and materialism. Seventy-three percent felt that limiting children's exposure to popular culture was "nearly impossible."[4]

That's the bad news. The good news is that evidence shows kids do still listen to their parents. In a 2000 survey by the YMCA, 84 percent of teen boys and 72 percent of teen girls said they turned to their parents for advice. And parents and teens reported spending about 80 minutes a day talking to one another. But parents still have some trouble getting their messages across. The survey found that while 64 percent of parents said they spoke often about values and beliefs with their children, only 41 percent of the teens agreed that they have these conversations frequently. Similarly, while 62 percent of parents "strongly agreed" that they share the same basic values with their teens, only 46 percent of the teens felt that way.[5]

So we as parents have some work to do to counter the effects of the toxic culture that threatens to engulf our kids. Here are more suggestions to help you shoulder that responsibility.

Make sure you *really* know what your child is reading, watching, and listening to.

As we've noted before, a lot of parents just aren't aware of all that their kids are consuming in the media. The YMCA survey found, for example, that although 85 percent of parents said they frequently monitor what their kids watched on TV, 61 percent of the children said they watched without any parental supervision. Also, 71 percent of parents claimed to frequently monitor their child's use of the Web, but 45 percent of the teens said they surfed the Web unsupervised often or all of the time. So if you need to keep better tabs on your child's media diet, you can do these things:

- Keep all computers and television sets in common areas of the house like family rooms and kitchens rather than in your child's bedroom.

- When your child is young, get in the habit of requiring him or her to ask for your permission to watch specific television programs and movies or to purchase video games and CDs. Look over the magazines your child is reading.

- Discourage or don't allow random channel surfing.

- Keep in touch with the parents of your child's friends. Discuss your kids' media habits with them, and see if you can come to some agreement about the kinds of TV shows, videos, video games, and music they are allowed to view or listen to when they are together.

- Make use of product warning labels and online and other resources available to parents to check on the content of new audio and video entertainment as it's released. If you're still unsure of its appropriateness, preview it yourself before letting your child see it. Be aware that although the Recording Industry Association of America (RIAA) has a labeling system to warn parents of explicit lyrics, it is voluntary. The RIAA estimates that less than one-half of one percent of sound recordings carry the parental advisory label. And most labels don't identify whether the explicit language is sexual, violent, or profane in nature.

- Keep discussions of what media your child is allowed to have access to as calm as you can. If you find your child watching something inappropriate, have a two-way conversation with him or her about it. Take this as a teaching opportunity. Talk about the content, why your child chose to view it, if he or she knows why you object to it, and what happens next (turning off the set, returning the product to the store, following through with a negative consequence, etc.).

Set clear media viewing rules for your child.

It's only fair to let children know in advance what they may and may not listen to or view. Set age-appropriate rules for your child, and sit down and discuss them with him or her. Be careful of setting a rule that depends purely on an outside rating system (for film or video game viewing, for example) that doesn't allow you any discretion based on the product's content. So you might want to tell your 15-year-old that he may attend any G- or PG-rated movie, but that he must still get your specific permission to see a PG-13 movie. It's also important to talk about the reasons for your rules and what will happen when rules are broken. Knowing the consequences for breaking the rules may encourage kids to follow them.

Use available technology to block objectionable media from entering your home.

Research shows that many parents still don't use the devices that can help them limit objectionable media content. For example, a 2001 Kaiser Family Foundation study found that of parents who know they have a V-chip in their TV that can lock kids out of programs with violent or sexual content only 36 percent choose to use it. But this device and other technology can be of significant help, especially to parents of young children. Filtering software can keep your child from viewing adult or porn sites on the Web. Other software enables you to check on the sites your child has visited on the Internet or the chat room and instant messaging discussions he or she has joined. For a fee, cable companies will block channels like MTV from your television sets. The V-chip on your TV can be used to lock kids out of viewing programming with violent or sexual content. For the latest information on using these measures, check with the organizations and Web sites listed in our "Resources for Parents" section.

Help your child be media literate and to put media content into appropriate context.

You need to be more than just a "media cop" to your child. Kids live in a media-saturated world. No matter how hard you try, you will never be able to screen your child from all objectionable media content. Other parents will not always share your concerns. Peer pressure may tempt your child to test or break your media rules. There is evidence that setting too-strict TV rules at home actually encourages older children to watch forbidden programs somewhere else. Researchers have found that talking with teens about issues rather than restricting their access to television was more likely to influence what they watched.

So you must help kids become media literate – able to question, evaluate, and make good decisions on their own about the media messages they encounter. The best thing you can do when you find your child has viewed something that is objectionable to you is to discuss it openly. What did your child think of it? Was it an accurate depiction of how people actually behave or how the world really is? What are the real-life consequences of violence or sexual activity?

Encourage or support media literacy courses in the school curriculum. PBS, the Center for Media Literacy, and other organizations have Web sites and videos that examine advertising techniques and media messages. They can demonstrate to kids how marketers can manipulate and even fake the images they present. If your child is nagging you to buy some new product, ask him how he learned of it. Ask him if he knows that the message posted on a Web site bulletin board or the product recommendation made by the cool kid in his class might actually have been planted and paid for by a marketer. You could make a game out of pointing to outrageous examples of marketing hype or spotting subtle, subliminal advertising messages in entertainment media.

If you have a daughter, it could be vital to her health and self-esteem to discuss advertising and media images of girls and women with her. Are these images like the real girls she sees every day? What damage could these images do to her and her friends? Make sure she knows that photos of models and celebrities can no longer be trusted to be "real." Computers can banish blemishes, bulges, and wrinkles. Ask her on what basis we judge other people and how we decide who our friends will be.

Another important ongoing discussion you should have with your children is about the male-female and family relationships that are portrayed in the media. What are the emotional, physical, and spiritual consequences of casual sex? Does the way we dress send messages to other people? What are the real-life dangers of wearing sexually provocative clothing? How do girls *want* to be treated by boys? How are they actually treated? What harm does vulgar language do to relationships? Why is it important to control our anger? How do parents and children show respect for each other? The list of topics you can talk over with your child is endless, and you can let the questions originate from the entertainment and marketing you view with your child.

Encourage your child to enjoy healthy entertainment and activity alternatives.

We've highlighted a lot of media content that you probably agree is appalling when it is viewed by or marketed to kids. We've done that to help make you aware of the worst that's available to young people. However, there are also plenty of wonderful programs and products out there that can make you and your child laugh, cry, think, question, learn, and appreciate. Stay on the lookout for them, and enjoy them together as a family whenever you can. Also support and encourage your child's participation in life-enhancing activities – outdoor recreation, sports, reading, volunteering, singing, playing a musical instrument, hobbies, drawing and painting, taking care of pets, growing a vegetable or flower garden. This list is just a start to the opportunities available.

Take personal action to help clean up the toxic media and marketing environment.

You can do more than just try to shelter your own child from junk entertainment and damaging advertising. Cultural change, says psychologist Mary Pipher, best-selling author of *Reviving Ophelia,* "is a million individual actions."[6] Write letters of complaint about

TV programming to the FCC. Join a children's advocacy group. Let marketers know when you find an ad objectionable or a product harmful to kids. Tell your legislators that you support laws that protect children. Complain to retailers when they sell kid-damaging products. Boycott the manufacturers of such products. In our opinion, this is not censorship; it's exercising your own First Amendment rights.

Sometimes it's disheartening to see that calling attention to marketing excesses or outrageous media actually spurs sales or increases the audience. But we need to set an example for our children and let them know that we believe that appropriate standards and boundaries help us lead healthy lives. Advertisers should be called to account when they venture past the limits of decency and good taste. And, occasionally, protests and complaints work! For example, Wal-Mart pulled a number of sexually explicit "laddie" magazines like *Maxim* and *Stuff* from its shelves when enough customers complained. Spurred by shopper protests, several department stores removed signage and logo-ed merchandise produced by French Connection United Kingdom, a merchandiser that has used its initials, "FCUK," to provocatively label and market its perfume and clothing to teenagers. Faced with growing consumer opposition, the company announced it would re-label its product without the offensive abbreviation for U.S. department stores.[7]

Although you can't control the larger cultural environment, you can create an "oasis" for your children in your own home.

Television sets, stereos, VCRs, CD and DVD players, and computers all come with "off" buttons. Don't be afraid to push them! Turn down the volume of pop culture by creating quiet zones and quiet times in your home when family members have time to read, play, think, and converse. This will encourage your kids to develop other resources and skills when they can't rely entirely on the media to keep them entertained. It will also give you the time to counter the damaging cultural messages every child faces. We hope this book has given you the incentive and the tools to become a more active influence in your child's life and relationships.

Appendix

Resources for Parents

There are many nonprofit organizations, governmental agencies, and advocacy groups concerned with issues regarding marketing, media, and children. We have listed many of them in this Resources section. Listing these organizations in this section does not imply that the authors agree with or endorse all of their material or conclusions.

General Media ···

(Information on advertising, marketing, and the Internet)

ACME: Action Coalition for Media Education
6400 Wyoming Blvd. NE, Albuquerque, NM 87109
(505) 828-3377

ACME Essential Resources Guide
http://www.acmecoalition.org/resources.html

This site offers a broad-ranging list of resources
about the media, including articles, Web sites, films, books,
magazines, and other resources. It recommends many
items for use by teachers who want to explore various
aspects and influences of the media in their classrooms.

Alliance for a Media Literate America

721 Glencoe St., Denver, CO 80220
(888) 775-2562 (toll-free)
http://www.amlainfo.org

This organization sends a free e-mail newsletter, holds a
national conference, and sponsors advocacy programs to
increase media literacy for children, parents, and teachers.

American Academy of Pediatrics

http://www.aap.org/family/ratingsgame.htm

On this site, parents get a specific explanation of the
current rating systems for movies, television programs,
video games, computer games, and music, and tips on how
to protect their children from harmful media messages.

Center on Alcohol Marketing and Youth

http://www.camy.org

The marketing of alcoholic beverages and its effect on
youth and underage drinking is the focus of the articles,
studies, and ad examples found on this site. Parents can
find valuable information about alcohol ads in magazines,
on television, and other media outlets.

Center for Media Education

2120 L St. NW, Suite 200, Washington, D.C. 20037
(202) 331-7833
http://www.cme.org

Parents can learn about Internet privacy for children, online marketing directed toward children, and technology aimed at protecting children from objectionable television programs among the entries on this site. The goal of the site is to ensure that the media serves the public interest.

Center for Media Literacy

3101 Ocean Park Blvd., #200, Santa Monica, CA 90405
(310) 581-0270
http://www.medialit.org

A resource catalog, and reports, articles, and news items on children and the media are among the features offered by this site. It also provides links to other sites and media areas, including faith-based media literacy.

Children Now

1212 Broadway, 5th Floor, Oakland, CA 94612
(510) 763-2444
Directory of Children's Issues on the World Wide Web:
Children & the Media
http://www.childrennow.org/links/links-media.html

A directory of links to media-oriented Web sites that cover issues ranging from advertising to children's programming is available on this site.

The Children's Partnership (TCP)

Welcome to the Information Superhighway
http://www.childrenspartnership.org/pub/pbpg98/
pguide98.html

This site provides a parents' guide to the "information superhighway" from information gathered from parent interviews. It also includes answers to the questions parents frequently ask about their children's use of the Internet and the World Wide Web.

The Coalition for Quality Children's Media and Kids First

112 West San Francisco St., Suite 305A,
Santa Fe, NM 87501
(505) 989-8076
http://www.cqcm.org/kidsfirst/home.shtml

Parents and children can search reviews for more than 3,000 films, videos, DVDs, audio recordings, TV programs, and CD-ROMs. The site's goal is to teach children critical viewing skills so they can make their own informed choices about what they watch, and to highlight quality children's programs.

Commercial Alert

4110 SE Hawthorne Blvd. #123, Portland, OR 97214
(503) 235-8012
http://www.commercialalert.org

Founded by Ralph Nader and Gary Ruskin, this nonprofit organization's mission is to "protect children and communities from commercialism." It publishes an e-mail newsletter, conducts public information campaigns, and lobbies Congress and governmental agencies on commercialism issues.

Common Sense Media

http://www.commonsensemedia.org/

The mission of the site is to give parents, educators, and kids "a choice and a voice about the media they consume." Articles on media products, from advertisements to CDs, as well as information on media studies and surveys are featured. Viewers are invited to rate products and express their opinions.

Family Safe Media

(800) 828-4514 (toll-free)
http://www.familysafemedia.com/

This online catalog features the most up-to-date electronic products that parents can buy to protect their children from profanity, violence, and sexual content contained in media entertainment. Items include channel and profanity blockers, TV time monitors, and Internet pornography filters.

Federal Communications Commission (FCC)

http://www.fcc.gov/cgb/complaints.html

Parents who want to file a complaint with the FCC about media activities will find the appropriate Web site, address, phone numbers, Fax number, and e-mail address at this site. The Consumer and Governmental Affairs Bureau operates the site.

The Henry J. Kaiser Family Foundation

2400 Sand Hill Road, Menlo Park, CA 94025
(650) 854-9400
http://www.kff.org

This site, entitled "Program for the Study of Entertainment Health and Media," presents articles, surveys, and fact sheets that address trends in parents' and children's perceptions and concerns about the media and other useful information.

Institute for American Values

1841 Broadway, Suite 211, New York, NY 10023
(212) 246-3942
The Motherhood Project
http://www.rebelmothers.org

The Motherhood Project promotes and encourages mothers to take a more active role in improving the quality of life for their children. One specific area where this can take place in regard to the media is teaching children the human values of a "mother world" over the material values of a "money world."

Internet Safety Watch, Inc.

Cyber Hood Watch
http://www.cyber-hood-watch.org/parent_resources.htm

This site promotes children's safety on the Internet by providing links to positive family Internet activities and technology that parents can use to screen and filter harmful messages.

Media Literacy Education for Parents & Kids

http://www.medialiteracy.com/parents/parents.htm

A list of resources, Internet links, books, videos, teaching kits, and other materials on the media are provided for parents, child-care providers, and early childhood educators. All materials are geared to help inform and educate adults about current media trends and actions parents and families can take to promote healthier media habits.

Mediascope

100 Universal City Plaza, Bldg. 6159,
Universal City, CA 91608
(818) 733-3180
http://www.mediascope.org

This nonprofit research and policy organization seeks to encourage responsible portrayals in film, television, the Internet, video games, music, and advertising. It offers publications for parents and educators and teams up with parent-teacher organizations to disseminate information about social issues in the media.

National Institute on Media and the Family

606 24th Ave. South, Suite 606, Minneapolis, MN 55454
(888) 672-5437 (toll free)
http://www.mediafamily.org

Media news and reviews of movies and video games are just two features of this site, designed to help families and educators maximize the benefits and minimize the harm of mass media on children through research, education and advocacy.

Parental Media Guide

http://www.parentalguide.org/

This is a "one-stop" Web site for parents who want to review the parental advisory systems for the movie, music, electronic game, and cable and broadcast television industries. It also provides answers to questions parents frequently ask about the systems.

Parenthood in America

http://www.parenthood.library.wisc.edu/Cantor/Cantor.html

Joanne Cantor, Ph.D., outlines some of the key points in her 1998 book, *Mommy, I'm Scared: How TV and Movies Frighten Children and What We Can Do to Protect Them.* The article touches on the long-term effects of frightening media images on young children, and how parents can respond to reassure kids.

Plugged In Online

http://www.pluggedinonline.com/

A Web site of Focus on the Family, this site focuses on media entertainment from a Christian perspective and is intended for use by parents, youth leaders, ministers, and teens. Reviews of current movies, television programs, music CDs, and video/DVDs provide specific information on sexual content, profanity, violence, and what lessons are taught in order to stimulate parent-teen or church group-teen discussions.

Public Broadcasting System
PBS Kids

Don't Buy It Guide for Parents and Caregivers
http://www.pbskids.org/dontbuyit/parentsguide.html

Helping parents help children understand the difference between real-life values and media entertainment is the goal of this site. Issues range from setting up a weekly family TV diary to the tricks of the trade advertisers use to introduce and sell products.

PBS Parents

Growing with Media
http://www.pbs.org/parents/issuesadvice/
growingwithmedia/gradeschool/dilemmas/index.html

Parents will find answers to a variety of daily dilemmas they may face when helping their children make good decisions about watching television and movies, using the Internet, and sorting through advertising messages. Parents also can ask their own questions on this site.

PBS TeacherSource

http://www.pbs.org/teachersource/media_lit/
related_study.shtm

This site offers links to dozens of Web sites with information on topics such as advertising and marketing practices, commercialism in schools, media violence, gender and media, news reporting, and video games. Although the site is designed for use by teachers, parents also can find helpful information on media trends and products.

Movies ....

Grading the Movies: Helping Families Find Entertainment with Values

http://www.gradingthemovies.com/

The main feature is movie reviews for parents and children based on an A-to-F grading system. Reviews summarize movies, past and present, and give letter grades in areas of overall quality, violence, sexual content, language, and drugs/alcohol.

Screen It!

http://www.screenit.com/index.html

Reviews of current and past movies, videos and DVDs, and music are presented to help parents determine appropriate forms of entertainment for their children. Movie reviews provide detailed information in areas such as profanity, drug and alcohol use, sex and nudity, violence, blood and gore, and frightening scenes.

The Movie Mom

http://www.movies.yahoo.com/moviemom

Author and media expert Nell Minow (the Movie Mom) reviews current movies and videos so that parents can decide which ones are suitable for their children, ages 2 to 18. The site also offers information to spur family discussions on media issues.

Music ....

Lyrics.com

http://www.lyrics.com

Parents can check lyrics from songs by hundreds of artists and bands, past and present. Artists are listed alphabetically; clicking on an artist brings up selected albums (not all albums for an artist are displayed), and lyrics for each song on the album are provided.

Songlyrics.com

http://www.songlyrics.co.nz/lyrics/b/index.htm

This site features song lyrics from many current artists in pop, rock, rap, and hip hop. Parents can search for artists alphabetically or click directly on an artist's name.

Song Lyrics

http://www.thesonglyrics.com/

Features on this site include a Top 30 list of artists whose lyrics are most requested and an Internet search box that enables parents to find Web sites with lists of lyric sites for specific artists.

Television

Educational Resources Information Center (ERIC)

2277 Research Blvd. MS 6M, Rockville, MD 20850
(800) 538-3742 (toll-free)
What Do Parents Need to Know About Children's Television Viewing?
http://www.eric.ed.gov/archives/tv.html

This article provides information for parents about how watching too much TV can affect children and provides tips on how to help develop healthier viewing habits.

Media Awareness Network (Canadian)

1500 Merivale Road, 3rd Floor, Ottawa,
Ontario K2E 6Z5

(800) 896-3342 (toll-free)
http://www.media-awareness.ca

With features for parents and teachers, this Canadian site promotes helping children become more media savvy through a variety of articles and discussion issues. One link explores the positive and negative sides of young people watching television and provides discussion topics and questions parents can use in teaching their children good viewing habits. (Also includes information on music, movies, the Internet, video games, and marketing.)

Parents Television Council

707 Wilshire Boulevard #2075, Los Angeles, CA 90017
(213) 629-9255
http://www.parentstv.org/

Ratings of television programs, articles and publications on television-related issues, and tips on taking action against objectionable TV content are just a few of the features of this site. It also provides a list of the best and worst primetime broadcast television programs for families and features such as cartoon and movie reviews.

Video Games ....

Daytrum – The Technology Guide for Families

http://www.daytrum.com/

Reviews of computer and video games, and computer software with an emphasis on family-oriented entertainment are the highlights of this site. Computer and video game reviews include a family-values and violence rating, and parental advisory information.

Entertainment Software Rating Board (ESRB)
Check the Rating
http://www.esrb.org/

The ESRB rating system, which helps parents and other consumers choose the games that are right for their families, is explained, and parents are shown how to use it. ESRB ratings include rating symbols that suggest what age group a game is best for and content descriptors that tell parents about content elements that may be of interest or concern. When parents check the ratings, control of children's video games is in their hands.

Parents Television Council
707 Wilshire Boulevard #2075, Los Angeles, CA 90017
(213) 629-9255
http://www.parentstv.org/ptc/video games/main.asp

This site provides an explanation of ESRB ratings for video games and lists appropriate games that are recommended for children of different age groups. Parents can look up ratings for specific video games, and articles identify games that contain violent and/or sexual content.

Notes

Chapter 1 ···

1. Lucian James, quoted in Gil Kaufman, "Push the Courvoisier," MTV.com, http://www.mtv.com/news/articles/147393/20030606/index.jhtml?headlines=true.

2. The Motherhood Project, Watch Out for Children: A Mother's Statement to Advertisers, Institute for American Values, 2002, pp. 23-24.

3. Naomi Klein, *No Logo*, New York: Picador, USA, 2002, p. 68.

4. Neil Howe and William Strauss, *Millennials Rising*, New York: Vintage Books, 2000, p. 265.

5. Jason Maltby, quoted in Richard Linnett, "Is Broadcast Ready for 'Coupling,'" *Advertising Age*, May 12, 2003.

Chapter 2 ···

1. Nancy Shalek, quoted in Ron Harris, "Children Who Dress for Success," *Los Angeles Times*, November 12, 1989.

2. Jon Hein, quoted in Olivia Barker, "Everything Is So 5 Minutes Ago," *USA Today*, June 10, 2003.

3. Paco Underhill, *Why We Buy: The Science of Shopping*, New York: Simon & Schuster, 1999, p. 144.

4. Peter Vilbig, "Advertising's Sneak Attack," *The New York Times Upfront Online*, http://www.nytimes.com/upfront/issue/April8,2002/13aads.htm.

5. James U. McNeal, Ph.D., *The Kids Market*, Ithaca, NY: Paramount Market Publishing, 1999, p. 81.

6. Allen Kanner, quoted in Miriam H. Zoll, "Psychologists Challenge Ethics of Marketing to Children," American News Service, viewed at http://www.mediachannel.org/originals/kidsell.shtml.

7. Tim Kassell, quoted in Zoll, "Psychologists Challenge."

Chapter 3 ....

1. Mike Searles and Carol Herman, quoted in The Motherhood Project, "Watch Out for Children: A Mother's Statement to Advertisers," Institute for American Values, 2002, pp. 12, 15.

2. Marion Nestle and Margo Wootan, quoted in The Food Institute Report, "Spending on Marketing to Kids Up $5 Billion in Last Decade," April 15, 2002.

3. Packaged Facts, "The U.S. Kids Market," 2002, available at http://www.marketresearch.com.

4. "Kidscreen Summit," viewed at http://www.kidscreen.com, June 26, 2003.

5. Center for a New American Dream, poll conducted July 20-21, 1999, http://www.newdream.org/campaign/kids/press-release.html.

6. Ibid.

7. Susan Linn and Diane E. Levin, "Stop Marketing 'Yummy Food' to Children," *The Christian Science Monitor,* June 20, 2002.

8. Arnold Aronson, quoted in Lorrie Grant, "Upscale Retailers Go Miniature to Draw Kids into Brand Loyalty," *USA Today,* September 24, 2003.

9. Michael McCarthy, "Reebok Signs Talented Kids Up," *USA Today,* May 21, 2003.

10. Mediascope, "Children, Health, and Advertising," http://www.mediascope.org/pubs/ibriefs/cha.htm.

11. Robert W. McChesney, "Oligopoly: The Big Media Game Has Fewer and Fewer Players," *The Progressive*, November 1999.

12. Jim Morelli, "Hooking Them Early," Web MD Medical News Archive, http://www.my.webmd.com/content/Article/30/1728_72898.htm.

13. The New Rules Project, "Curbing the Commercialization of Public Space," http://www.newrules.org/info/publicspace.html.

14. Mediascope, "Children, Health."

15. Anthony E. Gallo, "Food Advertising in the United States," U.S. Department of Agriculture, Economics Research Service, Food and Rural Economics Division, Agriculture Information Bulletin No. 750.

16. Andrew Lazar, quoted in Parija Bhatnagar, "Blue Food Blues," CNNMoney, http://www.cnn.com/2003/06/17/news/companies/failed_food/index.htm?cnn=yes.

17. Mediascope, "Children, Health."

18. Scott Leith, "Coke Won't Market Directly to Children," *The Atlanta Journal-Constitution*, July 19, 2003.

19. Susan Stock, "Swimming in Profits," *Lansing State Journal*, July 21, 2003.

20. Ibid.

21. Linn and Levin, "Yummy Food."

22. Theresa Howard, "Clifford Woofs Up Success," *USA Today*, April 28, 2003.

23. Jerome and Dorothy Singer, quoted in Claudia Kalb, "The End of Make Believe," *Newsweek International*, August 25, 2003.

24. Barbara Yost, "Kids Obesity a Call to Arms," *The Arizona Republic*, October 15, 2003.

Chapter 5 ··

1. Cynthia Peters, "Teacher, There's a Brand Name in My Math Problem," Znet Commentary, http://www.zmag.org/zsustainers/zdaily/1999%2D08/23peters.htm.

2. Karen van Kampen, "Tweens Trade Their Spaces – for $50,000," *National Post,* July 25, 2003.

3. East West Creative, "License to Thrill," *Buzz,* Summer 2003.

4. James McNeal, quoted in Heather Landy, "Kiddie Cash," *Fort Worth Star-Telegram,* October, 13, 2003.

5. Center for a New American Dream, poll, May 2002, http://www.newdream.org/campaign/kids/press-release2002.html.

6. Carter Kustera, quoted in Richard Linnett, "Adages," *Advertising Age,* June 2, 2003.

7. Center for Commercial-Free Public Education, "Channel One," http://www.commercialfree.org/channelone.htm.

8. Kenetta Bailey, quoted in Wayne Friedman, "Message Is Cool for School," *Advertising Age,* July 28, 2003.

9. Caroline E. Mayer, "It's a Jungle Out There in School Classrooms," *The Washington Post,* June 16, 2003.

10. Mike Blakeslee, quoted in Mayer, "It's a Jungle."

11. Dan Fuller, quoted in Mayer, "It's a Jungle."

12. Jean Kilbourne, quoted in Mayer, "It's a Jungle."

13. Roger Ebert, review of "The Lizzie McGuire Movie," *Chicago Sun-Times,* May 2, 2003.

14. Bruce Horovitz, "Just Can't Get Enough of Duff," *USA Today,* July 16, 2003.

15. Associated Press, "Olsen Twins: Teen Moguls Go Global," viewed at http://www.teenresearch.com/NewsView.cfm?page_id=128.

16. Laura Sessions Stepp, "Nothing to Wear," *The Washington Post,* June 3, 2002.

17. Kathy Bronstein, quoted in Leslie Earnest, "Tweens: From Dolls to Thongs," *Los Angeles Times,* June 27, 2002.

18. Joanne Arbuckle, quoted in Fahizah Alim, "Too Little, Too Soon," *The Sacramento Bee,* July 6, 2003.

19. Earnest, "Tweens, From Dolls."

20. Alim, "Too Little."

21. Earnest, "Tweens, From Dolls."

22. Lois Banner, quoted in Alim, "Too Little."

23. Scott Bracale, quoted in Bruce Horovitz, "More Parents Leave School Shopping to the Kids," *USA Today,* August 11, 2003.

24. Joline Godfrey, quoted in Horovitz, "More Parents Leave."

25. Product Placement Awards, http://www.productplacementawards.com/history.html.

26. Product Placement Awards, http://www.productplacementawards.com/latest.html.

27. Anita Stackhouse-Hite, "Beyond the Blackboard: Whatever It Takes to Get Kids to Read," *The Porterville Recorder,* July 25, 2003.

28. Mike Fisher, quoted in Gene Emery, "What's in a Name: Product Placement in Games," Reuters, January 30, 2002, viewed at http://www.usatoday.com/tech/techreviews/2002/1/30/spotlight.htm.

29. Ellen Edwards, "Plug (the Product) and Play," *The Washington Post,* January 25, 2003.

30. Ibid.

31. KidzEyes, "FAQs," http://www.kidzeyes.com/faq.htm.

32. Ibid.

33. Ibid.

34.   C & R Research, "Our Toolbox," http://www.crresearch.com/toolbox/kidz.asp.

Chapter 6 ....

1.   Linda Sonna, Ph.D., *The Everything Tween Book,* Avon, MA: Adams Media Corporation, 2003, p. 45.

2.   Linda Perlstein, interview in Sarah Carr, "Author Turns Pages on Preteen Years," *Milwaukee Journal Sentinel,* October 4, 2003.

3.   Sonna, *The Everything Tween,* p. 53.

4.   Michael S. Josephson, Val J. Peter, and Tom Dowd, *Parenting to Build Character in Your Teen,* Boys Town, NE: Boys Town Press, 2001, pp. 17-22.

5.   S. Holly Stocking, Diana Arezzo, and Shelley Leavitt, *Helping Kids Make Friends,* Allen, TX: Argus Communications, 1980, p. 19.

6.   Reese Witherspoon, quoted in Merle Ginsberg, "Nouveau Reese," *W,* September 2002.

7.   Greg Weaver, quoted in Michele Orecklin, "Selling Teen Spirit," *Time,* August 18, 2003.

8.   Michael M. Brown, quoted in Drew Bracken, "Few Teens Head Outdoors," *The Advocate,* July 21, 2003.

Chapter 7 ....

1.   Michael Wood, quoted in Peter Vilbig, "Advertising's Sneak Attack," *The New York Times Upfront Online,* http://www.nytimes.com/upfront/issue/April8,2002/ 13aads.htm.

2.   Center for Media Education, "Marketing to Children Harmful," October 18, 2000, http://www.cme.org/press/001018pr.html.

3. American Academy of Child & Adolescent Psychiatry, "Normal Adolescent Development: Middle School and Early High School Years," May 1997, http://www.aacap.org/web/aacap/publications/factsfam/develop.htm.

4. Teen Research Unlimited, "Teens Spent $170 Billion in 2002," February 17, 2003, http://www.teenresearch.com/PRview.cfm?edit_id152.

5. *Advertising Age,* "Cable 2003: MTV/MTV2/MTV.com," May 19, 2003.

6. Betty Frank, quoted in David Hiltbrand, "Teens Rule a Different Reality on TV," Knight Ridder News Service, March 31, 2003, viewed at http://www.the.honolulu advertiser.com/article/2003/Mar/31/il/il07a.html.

7. Jon Hein, quoted in Olivia Barker, "Everything Is So 5 Minutes Ago," *USA Today,* June 10, 2003.

8. Lev Grossman, "The Quest for Cool," *Time,* August 30, 2003.

9. Michael Wood, quoted in Elizabeth Canning Blackwell, "What Do Teens Really Want," *North Shore Magazine,* viewed at http://www.teenresearch.com/NewsViews.cfm?edit_id=60.

10. Brian Morrissey, "P & G Targets Teens with Viral Campaign," Internet Advertising Report, October 29, 2002, http://www.internetnews.com/IAR/article.php/1490041.

11. Ira Matathia, quoted in Alice Z. Cuneo, "Bud Uses 'Reject' Spots in Viral Play," *Advertising Age,* July 21, 2003.

12. Vilbig, "Advertising's Sneak Attack."

13. Ibid.

14. Ibid.

15. R. Larson, "Secrets in the Bedroom: Adolescents' Private Use of Media," *Journal of Youth and Adolescence,* 24(5), 1995, pp. 535-51.

16. Theresa Howard, "Ads Crank Up the Volume with Tunes," *USA Today,* August 10, 2003.

17. James Mahoney, quoted in Howard, "Ads Crank Up."

18. Jay Coleman, quoted in Marc Pollack, "Marketing Revolution Sweeps the Music Business," *Advertising Age,* July 28, 2003.

19. Jameel Haasan Spencer, quoted in Gil Kaufman, "Push the Courvoisier," MTV.com, June 9, 2003, http://www.mtv.com/news/articles/147393/20030606/ index.jhtml?headlines=true.

20. Damon Dash, quoted in Steven Isaac, "Embedded Ads Force Teens to Be More Savvy," *Plugged In,* May 2003.

21. Mark Humphrey, quoted in Isaac, "Embedded Ads."

22. Joseph Califano, quoted in Isaac, "Embedded Ads."

23. Roger Brashears, Jr., quoted in Associated Press, "Alcohol Ads Targeted at Black Kids?," June 20, 2003, viewed at http://www.msnbc.com/news/929184.asp?Ocv=HB10.

24. National Institute on Media and the Family, "Fact Sheet: Alcohol Advertising and Youth, http://www.mediaandthe family.org/facts/facts_alcohol.shtml.

25. Ibid.

26. L. Leiber, "Commercial and Character Slogan Recall by Children Aged 9 to 11 Years," Center on Alcohol Advertising.

27. J. Grube and L. Wallack, "Television Beer Advertising and Drinking Knowledge, Beliefs, and Intentions Among Schoolchildren," *American Journal of Public Health,* 84(2), 1994.

28. Leiber, "Commercial and Character Slogan."

29. Ira Teinowitz and Jon Fine, "Alcohol Ad Guidelines Could Cause Hangover," *Advertising Age,* September 15, 2003.

30. Diane Riibe, quoted in Chad Purcell, "OK of Gelatin Shots Draws Critics," *Omaha World-Herald,* September 23, 2003.

31. Paige Farmer and Andrea Warren, quoted in Karen Dandurant and Elizabeth Kenny, "Under the Influence," *Portsmouth Herald,* September 28, 2003.

32. Center for Media Education, "TeenSites.com: A Field Guide to the New Digital Landscape," December 2001, http://www.cme.org/teenstudy/index.html.

33. Ibid., p. 32.

34. Ibid., p. 29.

35. Ibid., p. 33.

36. Ibid., p. 3.

37. Robert Manning, quoted in Sharon Epperson, "How to Balance Teens, Credit Cards," CNBC, June 3, 2003, http://www.msnbc.com/news/920108.asp.

38. Consumer Debt Counseling and Consumer Credit Counseling Service – St. Louis, "Flood of Credit Card Offers Spills Over Onto Teens," February 18, 2003, http://www.cccsstl.org/pressreleasedetail.asp?ID=90.

39. Epperson, "How to Balance Teens."

Chapter 8 ···

1. David G. Myers, "Wealth, Well-Being, and the New American Dream," Center for a New American Dream, http://www.newdream.org/discuss.myers.html.

2. Ibid.

3. Ed Diener, "Frequently Asked Questions About Subjective Well-Being (Happiness and Life Satisfaction)," viewed at http://www.s.psych.uiuc.edu/~ediener/faq.html.

4. Students Against Destructive Decisions/Students Against Driving Drunk and Liberty Mutual Insurance Group, "Teens Today 2002."

Chapter 9 ....

1. Joel Weinshanker, quoted in Ann Marie Kerwin, "The Buzz: In the World of Kid Movies," *Advertising Age*, September 29, 2003.

2. Quentin Tarantino, quoted in "Marketing Violence," *San Francisco Chronicle,* October 21, 2003.

3. Media Awareness Network, "Violence in Media Entertainment," http://www.media-awareness.ca/english/issues/violence/violence_entertainment.cfm.

4. Center for Media and Public Affairs, "The Rude and the Crude: Profanity in Popular Entertainment," July 1999, http://www.cmpa.com/archive/rudeandcrude.htm.

5. Jay Landers, quoted in Joel Federman, Ph.D., "Rating Sex and Violence in the Media: Media Ratings and Proposals for Reform," Kaiser Family Foundation, November 2002, p. 3.

6. Ibid.

7. Federal Trade Commission, "FTC Releases Report on the Marketing of Violent Entertainment to Children," September 11, 2000, http://www.ftc.gov/opa/2000/09/youthviol.htm.

8. Federal Trade Commission, "FTC Releases Second Follow-Up Report on the Marketing of Violent

Entertainment to Children," December 5, 2001, http://www.ftc.gov/opa/2001/12/violence.htm.

9. Russ Britt, "Filmmakers Covet PG-13 as the Rating to Lock In," CBS Marketwatch, in *Omaha World-Herald,* August 10, 2003.

10. Ibid.

11. Roger Ebert, quoted in Andy Seiler, "PG-13 Is Secret to Film Success," *USA Today,* July 1, 2003.

12. *Los Angeles Times,* "Disney Loses Innocence with First PG-13 Rating," June 20, 2003, viewed at http://www.ajc.com/business/content/business/0603/ 20 disney.html.

13. Seiler, "PG-13 Is Secret."

14. Bob Smithouser, "50 Cent Keeps It Real," *Plugged In,* April 2003.

15. Rich Thomaselli, "Reebok Gambles on 50 Cent Investment," *Advertising Age,* June 16, 2003.

16. Steve Jones, "Carrying on the Gangsta Mystique," *USA Today,* May 22, 2003.

17. Douglas Rushkoff, quoted in Public Broadcasting System press release, "Merchants of Cool," February 5, 2001.

18. Malcolm Mayhew, "The Height of Hip-Hop," *Fort Worth Star-Telegram,* viewed at http://www.ohio.com/mld/ohio/entertainment/music/ 7012184.htm.

19. Rushkoff, quoted in Public Broadcasting System, "Merchants of Cool."

20. Bakari Kitwana, quoted in Jeffrey Meyer, "Hip-Hop Fashion Hits the Suburbs," *The Christian Science Monitor,* October 22, 2003.

21. Jim Hainey, quoted in Michael Hiestand, "Controversy Greets Converse's 'Weapon' Shoe," *USA Today,* September 25, 2003.

22. John Clarke, quoted in Dr Pepper Seven UP, Inc., press release, "2003 Dr Pepper, Diet Dr Pepper Ads Hit the Airwaves in January," viewed at http://www.dpsu.com/nr_dpads.html.

23. Chuck D, quoted in Steve Jones, "Difficult Debate Rages Behind Image's Appeal," *USA Today,* May 23, 2003.

24. Adrian Arceo, "Hip Hop Ya Don't Stop," http://www.allhiphop.com/editorial/?ID=142.

25. Sway Calloway, quoted in Smithouser, "50 Cent Keeps It Real."

26. Peter Lewis, "Videogames: The Biggest Game in Town," *Fortune,* September 2, 2003.

27. Jonathan Wendel, quoted in Fred Guterl, "Bionic Youth: Too Much Information," *Newsweek International,* August 25, 2003.

28. Lewis, "Videogames."

29. David Walsh, quoted in Loren Eaton and Bob Smithouser, "Navigating the Video Game Maze," *Plugged In,* March 2003.

30. Patricia Vance, quoted in Mike Snider, "Ratings to Be Clearer on Videogame Boxes," *USA Today,* June 26, 2003.

31. American Psychological Association, "Violence on Television – What Do Children Learn? What Can Parents Do?," APA Online, http://www.apa.org/pubinfo/violence.html.

32. Leonard Eron, quoted in American Psychological Association, "Violence on Television."

33. American Academy of Child and Adolescent Psychiatry, "The Influence of Music and Music Videos," http://www.aacap.org/web/aacap/publications/factsfam/musicvid.htm.

34. Guterl, "Bionic Youth."

35. J. DeGaetano and K. Bander, "Violent Video Games and Stimulus Addiction," viewed at http://www.media-awareness.ca/eng/med/class/teamedia/vidintro.htm.

Chapter 10 ....

1. Andy Seiler, "PG-13 Is Secret to Film Success," *USA Today,* July 1, 2003.

2. Public Broadcasting System press release, "Merchants of Cool," February 5, 2001.

3. Jean Kilbourne, *Killing Us Softly 3,* Northhampton, MA: Media Education Foundation, 2000.

4. Jon Fine, "Teen Title Crush Leads to Circ Cuts," *Advertising Age,* July 7, 2003.

5. Michelle Branch, quoted in Maria Neuman, "Keeping It Real," *Elle Girl,* September/October 2003.

6. Dina Sansing, "New on the Tube," *Seventeen,* October 2003.

7. Marian Thurm, "Sorry," *Seventeen,* October 2003.

8. Laura Shinn, "Girls Gone Wild," *Seventeen,* October 2003.

9. Answer Guy, "What's Up," *Seventeen,* October 2003.

10. Sophie, "Sophie's Dating World," *Elle Girl,* September/October 2003.

11. Jean Kilbourne, *Can't Buy My Love: How Advertising Changes the Way We Think and Feel,* November 2000, viewed at http://www.cantbuymylove.com/chapter1.html.

12. Ibid.

13. Peter Ligouri, quoted in Richard Huff, "Heating Up the TV Screen," *New York Daily News,* September 28, 2003.

14. Martin D. Franks, quoted in Huff, "Heating Up."

15. Kaiser Family Foundation, in Huff, "Heating Up."

16. Catherine Warburton-Scott, in Richard Linnett, "Is Broadcast Ready for 'Coupling'?," *Advertising Age,* May 12, 2003.

17. Demetrius Denham, quoted in James Ragland, "Name Doesn't Go Down Well," *Dallas Morning News,* October 24, 2003.

18. Jim Keyes, quoted in Theresa Howard, "Energy Drinks Get Their Hip-Hop On," *USA Today,* October 27, 2003.

19. B. J. Sigismund, "XXX-ceptable," Newsweek Web Exclusive, July 2, 2003, viewed at http://www.msnbc.com/news/93452.asp.

20. Lisa Napoli, "Kids Will Find It," MSNBC, August 9, 2000, http://www.msnbc.com/news/44385.asp.

21. Russell Scott Smith, "Porn Reborn," *New York Post,* September 25, 2003.

22. Irma Zandl, quoted in Lev Grossman, "The Quest for Cool," *Time,* August 30, 2003.

23. Reactorz Research, "What Do Kids and Parents Think," March 28, 2003, http://www.reactorzresearch.com/recent/20030328.html.

24. Anorexia Nervosa and Related Eating Disorders, Inc., viewed at http://www.anred.com/stats.html.

25. *Reveries Magazine,* "Cool News of the Day," July 15, 2003, http://www.reveries.com/coolnews/2003/july/jul_15.html.

26. Suzanne Smalley, "'This Could Be Your Kid,'" *Newsweek,* August 18, 2003.

Chapter 11 ....

1. Kay S. Hymowitz, "The Contradictions of Parenting in a Media Age," in *Kid Stuff: Marketing Sex and Violence to America's Children,* Diane Ravitch and Joseph P. Viteritti, eds., Baltimore: The Johns Hopkins University Press, 2003, p. 228.

2. Ibid., p. 233.

3. Marilyn Gardner, "The Power of 1," *The Christian Science Monitor,* October 15, 2003.

4. Deirdre Donahue, "'A Culture Purposefully Damaging,'" *USA Today,* October 1, 1998.

5. YMCA, "Talking with Teens: The YMCA Parent and Teen Survey Final Report," 2000, http://www.ymca.net/presrm/research/teensurvey.htm.

6. Mary Pipher, quoted in Donahue, "Culture Purposefully Damaging."

7. Jack Neff, "FCUK Abandons Abbreviation to Get Perfume Back in Stores," *Advertising Age,* November 24, 2003.